William Kirkpatrick

Cheerful songs

William Kirkpatrick

Cheerful songs

ISBN/EAN: 9783337264956

Printed in Europe, USA, Canada, Australia, Japan

Cover: Foto ©Thomas Meinert / pixelio.de

More available books at **www.hansebooks.com**

CHEERFUL SONGS.

—BY—

WM. J. KIRKPATRICK,

JNO. R. SWENEY, AND L. L. PICKETT.

—— ORDER OF ——

Publishing House of the Methodist Episcopal Church South,
Barbee & Smith, Agents. Nashville, Tenn.

— OR OF —

L. L. Pickett, Columbia, S. C.

PREFACE.

———◦|◦———

WHERE are many books of song in the market, but the editors of this work humbly trust that it has a mission in the world. They send it out with the prayer that many souls may be helped on towards the blessed Land of Song by it.

(2)

CHEERFUL SONGS.

Glory to the Lamb.

ISAAC WATTS.   WM. J. KIRKPATRICK.

1. Come let us join our cheer-ful songs With angels round the throne,
2. "Wor-thy the Lamb that died," they cry, "To be ex-alt-ed thus!"
3. Je - sus is wor-thy to re-ceive Hon-or and pow'r di - vine;
4. The whole cre-a - tion join in one, To bless the sa-cred name

Ten thousand thousand are their tongues, But all their joys are one.
"Wor-thy the Lamb!" our hearts reply, "For he was slain for us."
And blessings more than we can give, Be, Lord, for - ev - er thine.
Of him that sits up - on the throne, And to a - dore the Lamb.

CHORUS.

Glo - ry to the Lamb! Glo - ry to the Lamb! Glory to the Lamb of God.

Glo - ry to the Lamb! Glo - ry to the Lamb! Glory to the Lamb of God.

3

The Fountain From the Rock.

"He smote the Rock, that the waters gushed out, and the streams overflowed."—Ps. 78: 20.

F. E. Hewitt. L. L. Pickett.

1. I have come to the fountain that flows from the Rock, The Rock that was
2. While I drink of the fountain that flows from the Rock, Sweet peace, like a
3. There is strength at the fountain that flows from the Rock, For life ev - er-
4. I'll abide by the fountain that flows from the Rock, And sink 'neath its

smitten for me; For I heard a sweet voice gently speak to my soul, O
beau - ti - ful dove, Nestles down in my heart, while the Spirit divine, A-
last- ing is there; And the soul gains a power that will victory win, In
bright, cleansing waves ; All its waters are sparkling with heavenly light; Our

CHORUS.

come to the wa - ters so free. O won - der- ful fount- ain that
wak - ens the mu - sic of love.
hours of temp-ta - tion and care.
Je - sus a - bun- dant- ly saves.

flows from the Rock, What tides of sal - va - tion out-pour! 'Tis for

you, 'tis for me, hal- le - lu - jah! Take free-ly, and thirst nevermore.

Him that Cometh unto Me. 5

E. E. HEWITT.　　　　　　John vi. 37.　　　　　WM. J. KIRKPATRICK.

1. Listen to the blessed invitation, Sweeter than the notes of angel-song,
2. Weary toiler, sad and heavy-laden, Joyfully the great salvation see,
3. Come, ye thirsty, to the living waters, Hungry, come and on his bounty feed,

Chiming softly with a heavenly cadence, Calling to the passing throng.
Close beside thee stands the Burden Bearer, Strong to bear thy load and thee.
Not thy fitness is the plea to bring him, But thy pressing utmost need.

CHORUS.

Him that cometh unto me, unto me, Him that cometh unto me,
unto me,

Him that cometh un-to me, un-to me, I will in no wise cast out.

4 "Him that cometh," blind or maimed or sinful
Cometh for his healing touch divine,
For the cleansing of the blood so precious,
Prove anew this gracious line.

5 Coming humbly, daily to this Saviour,
Breathing all the heart to him in prayer; [mansions
Coming some day to the heavenly
He will give thee welcome there.

6 Revive the Hearts of All.

JAMES L. BLACK. JNO. R. SWENEY.

1. God is here, and that to bless us With the Spirit's quick'ning power:
2. God is here! we feel his presence In this con - se - crat-ed place;
3. God is here! oh, then, believ - ing, Bring to him our one de- sire,
4. Saviour, grant the prayer we of- fer, While in sim - ple faith we bow,

See, the cloud alread - y bend- ing, Waits to drop the grateful shower.
But we need the soul-re- fresh-ing Of his free, unbounded grace.
That his love may now be kindled, Till its flame each heart inspire.
From the windows of thy mer - cy Pour us out a blessing now.

CHORUS.

Let it come, O Lord, we pray thee, Let the shower of blessing fall;
Let it come, Let the shower

We are wait - ing, we are waiting, Oh, revive the hearts of all.
We are waiting, Oh, re- vive

How are You Living?

Rev. E. A. Hoffman.   R. M. McIntosh.   By per.

1. How, oh, how are you liv-ing, my brother? Are you go-ing the pil-
2. Earth will offer you pleasures, my brother, Have you turn'd from these pleas-
3. Sin will sure-ly en-tice you, my brother, Quickly turn from tempta-
4. You may grow cold and careless, my brother, And from Christ and his fol-

grim-age way? Are you do-ing the will of your Mas-ter? Are you
ures a-way? Are you striving to work for the Mas-ter? Are you
tion a-way; O then give all your life to the Mas-ter, And be
low-ing stray; Are you watching and praying and trust-ing? Are you

REFRAIN.

liv-ing for Je-sus to-day? Are you liv-ing for Je-sus to-

day, to-day? Are you liv-ing for Je-sus to-day? O tell me, my friend

and my broth-er, Are you liv-ing for Je-sus to-day?

Trusting in the Name of Jesus.

CARRIE M. WILSON.   JNO. R. SWENEY.

1. In perfect peace I now can say, Trusting in the name of Je - sus, I
2. I came with guilt and sin oppressed, Trusting in the name of Je - sus, I
3. Beneath the hallowed mercy-seat, Trusting in the name of Je - sus, I

walk with God from day to day, Trusting in the name of Je - sus; I
took his yoke and found sweet rest, Trusting in the name of Je - sus; How
sit en - raptured at his feet, Trusting in the name of Je - sus; And

walk by faith and not by sight, Trusting in the name of Je - sus, His
light my burdens now ap - pear, Trusting in the name of Je - sus; I
when my span of life is o'er, Trusting in the name of Je - sus, My

Fine.

love my theme from morn till night, Trusting in the name of Je - sus.
have no time for doubt or fear, Trusting in the name of Je - sus.
soul shall fly to yon - der shore, Trusting in the name of Je - sus.

D. S.—walk with God from day to day, Trusting in the name of Je - sus.

CHORUS.   *D. S.*

Trusting in the name of Je - sus, On - ly in the name of Je - sus, I

Dear Saviour, Cleanse Me Now.

FRANK GOULD.　　　　　　　　　　　　　　　　　　　JNO. R. SWENEY.

1. A trembling soul I come to thee, And, if there yet is room for me In
2. I come in sim-ple faith alone, To plead thy merits,—not my own; I
3. I long to feel thy power divine, To see thy light around me shine, And
4. My life and breath, my heart and soul, I gladly yield to thy control; Oh,

yon - der fount so full and free, Dear Saviour, cleanse me now.
lay my heart be-fore thy throne, Dear Saviour, cleanse me now.
know henceforth that I am thine, Dear Saviour, cleanse me now.
let the heal - ing wa - ters roll, Dear Saviour, cleanse me now.

CHORUS.

Cleanse me now, cleanse me now, Bles - sed Saviour, cleanse me now; A

trembling soul I come to thee, Dear Saviour, cleanse me now.

Send Me.

Rev J. E. Rankin, D. D.

Rev. L. L. Pickett.

1. Are there those around my door, Whom I thoughtless do not see,
2. Are there those who're far from home, Far from home, O Lord, and thee?
3. Are there those who wretched hide, Sunk in sin to low de-gree,
4. Are there those who know thee not, On some isl- and of the sea?
5. Send me where thou knowest best, Where the greatest need may be;

Sick, neg-lect - ed, wretched, poor, From their sin and suff'ring sore?
O'er the wilds who law- less roam, 'Neath the white Si - er - ras' dome?
On some cit - y's surg-ing tide, Lost to love and truth and pride?
In some lone, neg- lect - ed spot, Stained by many a sin and blot?
Where men are the most un- blest, Tossed up - on their sin's un- rest:

ad lib.

CHORUS.

Here am I, O Lord, send me. Send me, send me, Here am

Send me, send me,

I, O Lord, send me. Send me, send me, Here am I, O Lord, send me.

Send me, send me,

E. E. HEWITT.

JNO. R. SWENEY.

1. Good news! good news of a soul redeemed, A pen-i-tent for-giv-en! Good
2. Good news! good news that another heart Has learned redemption's story; Good
3. Good news! good news that another life Will show the power of Je - sus, Will
4. Good news! good news that another hand Will precious seed be sow-ing, An-

news! good news that an - oth - er friend is on the way to heav - en!
news! good news that an - oth - er voice will sing his praise in glo - ry.
prove the might of the sav - ing grace Which daily, hour- ly frees us.
oth - er guide to lead straying feet Where living streams are flowing.

CHORUS.

Rejoice! rejoice! there's joy to-day In the land beyond the riv - er; An-

oth - er gem for His di - a - dem, A star to shine for - ev - er.

Resting by and by.

Rev. W. E. Penn.   Chas. Edw. Pollock.

1. Christians, are you growing weary? There'll be resting by and by;
2. Have you man - y hours of anguish? There'll be resting by and by,
3. Cheer up, then, no long- er fearing, There'll be resting by and by,
4. Let us work, and keep on praying, There'll be resting by and by;

Is your pathway dark and dreary? There'll be resting by and by.
Where your souls will no more languish; There'll be resting by and by.
When you see our Lord's appearing; There'll be resting by and by.
If we come, His word o - beying; There'll be resting by and by.

REFRAIN.

There'll be resting by and by, There'll be resting by and by,

When the toils of life are o - ver, There'll be resting by and by.

From "Harvest Bells," by per.

Then Rejoice, all Ye Ransomed. 13

" There is joy in the presence of the angels of God, over one sinner that repenteth " Luke xv. 10.
E. F. M.   E. F. MILLER.

1. There's re - joicing in the presence of the an - gels O - ver
2. Oh, how happy is the sinner who has tast - ed Of the
3. In the home where once was strife and pain and sorrow, There'll be
4. We will ral - ly round the standard of our Sav - iour, And to

sinners coming home, . All the heav'nly harpers, with a mighty
Saviour's wond'rous love, Love that bringeth peace and joy, which passeth
blessed peace and joy, . Prayer and praise to God around the family
oth-ers loud-ly call, . Come, ye sinners, and repent, believe in
coming home,

D. S.—dead's alive, the lost is found, and
Fine. CHORUS.

chorus, Now are praising round the throne. Then rejoice, . . all ye
knowledge, Ever giv-en from a - bove.
al - tar Will the pow'r of sin destroy.
Je - sus, He will freely pardon all.   then rejoice,

wand'rers Now are coming, coming home.

D. S.

ran- somed, Let your praises reach to heaven's highest dome, For the
all ye ransomed,   highest dome.

From the " Shout of Victory By per."

Follow Me.

T. C. O'K.   T. C. O'Kane.

1. Hear you not the Saviour calling, Calling you so earnest - ly?
2. Lay not up on earth your treasure, Transient, perish - ing 'twill be;
3. In my Father's house in heaven, Let your hearts untroubled be,

Gent- ly, too, the tones are fall- ing, "Come, oh, come, and follow me."
Rath- er seek e - ter- nal pleasure; Would you find it? follow me.
Glorious man- sion will be giv - en, On - ly come and follow me.

CHORUS.

Let us round our Leader ral - ly, Je - sus bids us each to come;

He will lead us thro' the val - ley, O'er the riv - er, safe- ly home.

Be thy pathway bright or dreary
    Whither duty leadeth thee,
Strong thy steps, or faint and weary,
    I will guide thee,—follow me.

5 When thy days on earth are ending,
    And the close of life you see,
Even to the grave descending,
    Never fear, but follow me.

By permission.

Gather Them In.

Rev. Henry Burton. M.A.

Wm. J. Kirkpatrick.

1. Gath- er them in at the Master's call To the banquet of his love;
2. Gath- er them in, the halt and lame, By the winning word and deed;
3. Gath- er them in, there's none so low But the Lord shall bid him "Rise;"
4. Gath- er them in, the young and old, For the Father's love is free;
5. Then as the blood-washed raise their songs To the Lamb upon the throne,

Go bring them in, there's room for all In the Father's house above.
There is healing still in the wondrous name, And a help for every need.
There is none so sunk in the deeps of woe But may climb the highest skies!
For each and all there's a harp of gold, And a house by the jasper sea.
As you hear the harps of the countless throngs Their joy will swell your own·

CHORUS.

Go then and tell them, go and compel them, Gather them out of the mire of sin;

Go then and tell them, go and compel them, Gather them in, O gather them in!

Mrs. MARY D. JAMES.   **All Bright Above.**   WM. J. KIRKPATRICK

1. I see the bright, ef - fulgent rays Out beaming from the Saviour's face;
2. Oh, blessed vision! glad surprise! It breaks upon my wond'ring eyes,—
3. Triumphant Christ! all conqu'ring King! Thy praises I delight to sing;

No dark'ning clouds obscure the sight Of his sweet smile—my Life, my Light.
The Sun of Righteousness divine, In whom the Father's glories shine.
Thy glo - ry shines around me here, My path is bright, my sky is clear.

REFRAIN. *Not too fast.*

I am mounting on wings, I am soaring on high. Where the sun's ever shining in

unclouded sky, In the joy of his presence, the smiles of his love ; Oh,

glo - ry to Je - sus! 'tis all bright above ; 'Tis all bright above, 'tis *ad lib.*

all bright a-bove, Oh, glo - ry to Je - sus! 'tis all bright a-bove.

According to Your Faith.

Rev. J. L. STOKES.   L. L. PICKETT.

1. Blest Saviour, what a word is this! My heart leaps as   I   read;
2. It claims our Father's boundless store, The rich - es   of   his   grace,
3. Par - don and peace and ho - li - ness, And heav-en's own   re - ward,—
4. All, all is ours by sim - ple faith, Nothing have we   to   do,

'Tis all the strength, the love, the bliss We wea - ry sin - ners   need.
Greater than angel's thought, and more Than an - gel's hand can   trace.
Saviour, as - ton - ished, we con - fess Nev - er was such a   word.
But rest on what the Sa-viour saith, And find his word is   true.

REFRAIN.

"Ac - cord - ing to your faith" Is what the Sa - viour saith;

Lord, I be - lieve, And now re-ceive Ac-cord - ing to my   faith.

Beautiful Day.

W. J. K.

WM. J. KIRKPATRICK.

1. Beauti- ful day, lovely thy light; Ho- ly each ray, banishing night;
2. Beauti- ful day, calm was thy dawn; Joyous the lay, blessed the morn,
3. Beauti- ful day, perfect- ly bright; Jesus alway, boundless delight,
4. Beauti- ful day, haven of rest; Ev'ry one may come and be blest;

Cloudless thy sky; peaceful my stay Here in the sunlight of beautiful day.
When in my heart, over my way First shone the noontide of beautiful day.
Bliss all around, heaven by the way, Shining in fulness, oh, beautiful day!
Glory to God! naught can dismay ; Christ is the light of this beautiful day.

REFRAIN.

Beautiful, beautiful day,
Beauti - ful, beauti- ful day,

Evermore shine on my way;
Evermore shine on my way;

Saviour, I pray, keep me alway Safe in this beautiful day.

beau-ti - ful day.

What a Wonderful Saviour!

"And his name shall be called Wonderful."—Isa. ix. 6.

E. A. H.   ELISHA A. HOFFMAN. by per.

1. Christ has for sin atonement made, What a wonder — ful Saviour!
2. I praise him for the cleansing blood, What a wonder - ful Saviour!
3. He cleansed my heart from all its sin, What a wonder-ful Saviour!
4. He walks beside me in the way, What a wonder - ful Saviour!

We are redeemed! the price is paid! What a wonderful Saviour!
That reconciled my soul to God; What a wonder - ful Saviour!
And now he reigns and rules therein, What a wonder- ful Saviour!
And keeps me faithful day by day; What a wonder - ful Saviour!

CHORUS.

What a won - der - ful Sav - iour is Je - sus, my Je - sus!

What a won - der - ful Sav - iour is Je - sus, my Lord!

5 He gives me overcoming power,
  What a wonderful Saviour!
And triumph in each conflict hour,
  What a wonderful Saviour!

6 To him I've given all my heart,
  What a wonderful Saviour!
The world shall never share a part,
  What a wonderful Saviour!

I Want to be a Worker.

1. I want to be a worker for the Lord, I want to love and trust his holy
2. I want to be a worker ev-'ry day, I want to lead the erring in the
3. I want to be a worker strong and brave, I want to trust in Jesus' pow'r to
4. I want to be a worker; help me, Lord, To lead the lost and erring to thy

word; I want to sing and pray, and be bu-sy ev-'ry day In the
way That leads to heav'n above, where all is peace and love In the
save; All who will tru-ly come, shall find a hap-py home In the
word That points to joy on high, where pleasures never die In the

CHORUS.

1. vineyard of the Lord.   I will work,   I will pray,   In the
2, 3, 4. kingdom of the Lord.   I will work and pray, I will work and pray,

vineyard, in the vineyard of the Lord; of the Lord; I will work, I will

pray, I will la-bor ev-'ry day In the vineyard of the Lord.

Whatsoever.

J. A. HOLLAND.   Rev. L. L. PICKETT.

1. What - so - ev - er, in my name Ask, and thou receiv'st the same;
2. Is thy heart bowed down with sin? Je - sus longs to en - ter in;
3. Hast thou wandered from thy God? And deserv'st his chast'ning rod?

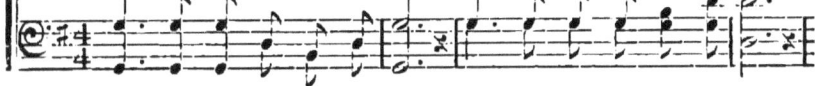

What - so - e'er thou dost require, Faith in Christ gains thy de - sire.
Longs to take thy load a - way, Longs to purge thy soul to - day.
Go to him on bended knee, Ask in faith, he'll par - don thee.

CHORUS.

In the Saviour's precious name All our prayers shall of - fered be,

And his grace shall answer give, If our faith but bring the plea.

4 Is tny soul with sorrow riven?
  And in vain with it hast striven?
  Carry all to God in prayer;
  Thou shalt be of heaven an heir.

5 Is thy life with care oppressed?
  Liv'st thou even in distress?
  Jesus Christ, the man of grief,
  Gives, to all who seek, relief.

6 Wilt thou by his hand be led?
  And by waters still be fed,
  Drinking draughts of grace divine?
  Live then always in the Vine.

7 May our trust from day to day
  Gleam, O Lord, with brightest ray,
  Till we see thee face to face,
  Perfect in thy power and grace.

Come Home.

I will arise and go to my Father."—Luke 15 : 18.

W. F. Cosner.   Chas. Edw. Pollock. By per.

1. The Sa - viour in - vites you, poor wand'rer, to come, The Fa - ther is
2. Re - turn to the Fa - ther, who holds you so dear; Say, why will you
3. Poor wan - der - er, haste, for the night draweth nigh ; Say, why will you
4. Come home, trembling mourner, oh, come and be blest, Here lay down your

wait - ing to wel - come you home ; Now cease from your wand'rings so
per - ish when plen - ty is near? Oh, leave the lone des - ert where
lin - ger still? Why will you die? Tho' poor and un - worth - y, with
bur - dens that you may find rest; Be cleansed from your sins, and to

lone - ly and wild; Re - turn to your Fa - ther, O prod - i - gal child!
shadows are piled; Re - turn to your Fa - ther, O prod - i - gal child!
sin all de - filed; The Fa - ther will wel - come his prod - i - gal child!
God re - conciled; Re - turn to your Fa - ther, O prod - i - gal child!

CHORUS.   *Repeat Chorus pp.*

Come home,   come home,   O prod - i - gal child, come home!
Come home,   come home,

Trusting Only Thee.

FRANCES RIDLEY HAVERGAL.   Words of Cho. by W. J. K.   WM. J. KIRKPATRICK.

1. I am trusting thee, Lord Je - sus, Trust-ing on - ly thee!
2. I am trusting thee for par - don, At thy feet I bow;
3. I am trusting thee for cleans - ing In the crim - son flood;
4. I am trusting thee to guide me; Thou a - lone shalt lead,

Trust - ing thee for full sal - va - tion, Great and free.
In thy grace and ten - der mer - cy Trust - ing now.
Trust - ing thee to make me ho - ly By thy blood.
Ev - 'ry day and hour sup - ply - ing All my need.

CHORUS.

I am trust - ing, trust - ing, Trust-ing on - ly thee;
I am trust - ing thee, trust - ing thee,

Sav - iour, Sav - iour, Trust - ing on - ly thee.
Trust - ing thee, trust - ing thee,

5 I am trusting thee for power,
    These can never fail;
Words that thou thyself shalt give me
    Must prevail.

6 I am trusting thee, Lord Jesus;
    Never let me fall;
I am trusting thee for ever,
    And for all

Jesus Waits to Help You.

Rev. E. A. Hoffman.   Wm. J. Kirkpatrick.

1. Broth - er, leave the path of sin, Je - sus waits to help you;
2. Broth - er, be no more a slave, Je - sus waits to help you;
3. Broth - er, come and join our band, Je - sus waits to help you;
4. Broth - er, will you still de - lay? Je - sus waits to help you;

He can break the bands with- in, Je - sus waits to help you.
Per - fect free - dom you may have, Je - sus waits to help you.
He will lead you by tho hand, Je - sus waits to help you.
Take a stand for right to - day, Je - sus waits to help you.

CHORUS.

Vic - to - ry! vic - to - ry! Glorious, glorious vic - to - ry!

Christ will break the tempter's power, Give you viet'ry from this hour.

A. S. KIEFFER.

D. E. DORTCH.

1. Oh, the night of Time soon shall pass a - way, And the
2. Oh, the hap - py day that shall gild the hills, When the
3. What a joy - ful time when the earth shall gleam In the

hap - py, gold - en day will dawn, When the pil - grim staff shall be
Lord shall come to earth a - gain! Oh, the hap - py hearts that shall
light of an e - ter - nal day, When the saints shall sing un - to

D. S.—We are wait - ing still for the

Fine. CHORUS.

laid a - side, And the king - ly crown put on. We are watching
welcome him When he comes once more to reign!
Christ, their King, In their gold - en, glad ar - ray!

Saviour, Christ, Who shall call his children home.

D. S.

now for the Morning Light, For the New Je - ru - salem to come;

What Wilt Thou have Me to Do?

CLAVES

WM. J. KIRKPATRICK. By per.

1. Are you willing, my sister, my brother, To work in the field of the Lord?
2. Say not, I am humble and lowly, And little can do if I would;
3. Do you pray to the "Lord of the harvest," That he would more laborers send,

Would you gladly choose more than another, His service to gain his reward?
Remember that Jesus, the Holy, Said of one, " She hath done what she could."
To fields that from you are the farthest, Neglecting those you should have gleaned?

Seek not for a prominent sta-tion, Your zeal or your ta-lent to show;
Some names shall, like stars, shine forever, Which few of this world ever knew;
Cease not in the earnest pe - ti - tion, For the laborers truly are few,

But ask in some humble re- lation, " Lord, what wilt thou have me to do?"
They sought with most earnest endeavor, " Lord, what wilt thou have me to do?"
Remembering to make this addition, " Lord, what wilt thou have me to do?"

REFRAIN.

What wilt thou have me to do, Lord? What wilt thou have me to do?

I ask, seeking guidance from heaven, Lord, what wilt thou have me to do?

Sweetly Resting.

Mary D. James

W. Warren Bentley.
By per.

1. In the rift - ed Rock I'm rest - ing, Safely sheltered I a - bide,
2. Long pursued by sin and Sa - tan, Weary, sad, I longed for rest;
3. Peace which passeth understanding, Joy the world can never give,
4. In the rift - ed Rock I'll hide me, Till the storms of life are past,

There no foes nor storms molest me, While within the cleft I hide.
Then I found this heav'nly shel - ter, Opened in my Saviour's breast.
Now in Je - sus I am find - ing: In his smiles of love I live.
All se - cure in this blest ref - uge, Heeding not the fiercest blast.

REFRAIN.

Now I'm rest - ing, Sweetly rest - ing, In the cleft once made for me;

Je - sus, blessed Rock of A - ges, I will hide my - self in thee.

T. C. O'KANE.   By per.

1. On Jor-dan's storm-y banks I stand, And cast a wish-ful eye
2. O'er all these wide- ex - tend - ed plains Shines one e - ter - nal day;
3. When shall I reach that hap - py place, And be for - ev - er blest?
4. Filled with delight, my rap - tured soul Would here no long - er stay;

To Canaan's fair and hap - py land, Where my pos - ses - sions lie.
There God the Son for - ev - er reigns, And scat-ters night a - way.
When shall I see my Father's face, And in his bo - som rest?
Tho' Jordan's waves a - round me roll, Fear - less I'd launch a - way.

CHORUS.

We will rest in the fair and happy land, Just across on the evergreen shore,. . .
by and by,   evergreen shore.

Sing the song of Moses and the Lamb, by and by, And dwell with Jesus evermore.

The Saviour Precious.

29

JAMES S. APPLE.   JNO. R. SWENEY.

1. I have found the Saviour precious, And I love him more and more;
I have found the Saviour precious, And I find him precious still;
2. I have found the Saviour precious, And, wherev-er I may go,
I am read-y, if he calls me, In the bat-tle front to stand;

He has rolled a-way my bur-den, And my mourning days are o'er;
All my life is con-se-crat-ed To his . . . . .
I will bear the roy-al standard, And its col-ors I will show;
I am read-y—yes, and waiting—To ful- - - - - .

service and his will. I have ta - - - ken up the cross, And will
fil my Lord's command. I have taken up the cross, And will nev-er lay it down, I have

CHORUS.

nev - - er lay it down Till I see . . . . his face in
taken up the cross, And will nev-er lay it down Till I see his face in glo-ry, 'Till I

glo - - - ry, And re-ceive . . . . a star-ry crown
see his face in glo-ry, And re-ceive a star-ry crown, a star-ry crown.

3 I have found the Saviour precious;
Hallelujah! praise his name!
To a mansion in his kingdom
Through his grace the right I claim.

I have found the Saviour precious;
He has proved my dearest Friend;
And my faith can trust his promise
Of protection to the end.

Copyright, 1888, by Jno. R. Sweney.

I'm Happy, so Happy!

LIZZIE EDWARDS.

JNO. R. SWENEY.

1. I'm happy, so happy! no words can express The joy and the comfort I see,
2. I'm happy, so happy! while trusting in him Whose presence o'ershadows my way;
3. My love may be tested, my faith may be tried, The depth of its fervor to prove,
4. O blessed Redeemer, some day I shall stand O'erwhelmed with the light of thy face,

For Jesus hath purchased, thro' infinite grace, A perfect salvation for me.
Who leadeth my soul by the river of peace, And giveth me strength as my day.
But welcome each trial, my Saviour designs The gold from the dross to remove.
Adoring forever, and shouting thy praise, Because thou hast saved me by grace.

CHORUS.

Saved, saved, oh, glo-ry to God! I feel the as-surance di-vine;

Saved, saved, oh, glo-ry to God! His Spir-it bears witness with mine.

Cast thy Bread upon the Waters.

W. J. K.

1. Cast thy bread up-on the wa-ters, Ye who have but scant supply,
2. Cast thy bread up-on the wa-ters, Poor and weary, worn with care,—
3. Cast thy bread up-on the wa-ters, Ye who have a-bundant store;
4. Cast thy bread up-on the wa-ters, Far and wide your treasures strew,
5. Cast thy bread up-on the wa-ters, Waft it on with praying breath,

An - gel eyes will watch above it;— You shall find it by and by!
Oft - en sitting in the shadow, Have you not a crumb to spare?
It may float on man-y-a bil-low, It may strand on many-a shore;
Scat - ter it with willing fin-gers, Shout for joy to see it go!
In some distant, doubtful moment It may save a soul from death;

He who in his righteous balance Doth each human ac-tion weigh
Can you not to those around you Sing some lit-tle song of hope,
You may think it lost for-ev - er, But, as sure as God is true,
For if you do close-ly keep it, It will on - ly drag you down;
When you sleep in solemn silence, 'Neath the morn and evening dew,

Will your sac - ri - fice remem-ber, Will your loving deeds re - pay.
As you look with longing vision Thro' faith's mighty tel - e-scope?
In this life or in the oth - er, It will yet return to you.
If you love it more than Je-sus, It will keep you from your crown.
Stranger hands, which you have strengthened, May strew lilies over you.

Lost but Found.

F. J. C.

JNO. R. SWENEY.

1. Oh, the joy that fills my heart! Oh, the grateful tears that start, When I
2. Lost but found, oh, wondrous thought! To his fold in mercy brought; Saved by

think . . of Je- sus' love! . . How he came that he might bear All my
When I think   Jesus' love!

grace, . . his grace di- vine; . . Heir with him of bliss untold, Soon his
Saved by grace,   grace divine;

weight of sin and care, How he came . . . from heav'n a -bove.
How he came   from heav'n a- bove.

glory I'll behold, What a bless - - ed hope is mine!
What a blessed hope is mine, What a blessed hope is mine

CHORUS.

Endless praise, endless praise   To the Lord . . my soul shall raise;
To the Lord,   my soul shall raise!

Lost but found, O happy strain! Dead but now . . I live a - gain.
Lost but found,   O happy strain! Dead but now I live, but now I live again, live again.

3 Lost but found! I now can sing
  Vict'ry through my Saviour King,
  ‖: Vict'ry ev'ry day and hour ; :‖
  Vict'ry still will be my song
  When I join the ransom'd throng,
  ‖: Vict'ry o'er the tempter's power. :‖

4 O that all the world would prove
  How a pard'ning God can love,
  ‖: How he waits for all who come! :‖
  O that all the world might see
  What his grace hath done for me!
  ‖: How he welcomes wand'rers home.:‖

Go Tell the World of His Love.

ABBIE MILLS.

WM. J. KIRKPATRICK.

1. Heirs to the kingdom of Jesus the Lord, Go tell the world of his love;
2. Think how he labored that we might have rest, Go tell the world of his love;
3. Plead to the lost ones to come while they may, Go tell the world of his love;

Publish the blessings that flow from his word, Go tell the world of his love;
Think how he suffered that we might be bless'd, Go tell the world of his love:
Jesus is waiting, he'll save them to-day, Go tell the world of his love:

Love that has purchas'd redemption from sin, Love that makes happy the spirit within
Sav'd by his mercy, upheld by his care, Tell of the goodness we constantly share;
Love that is nearest when earth joys are past, Lighting our pathway by clouds overcast;

Fine.

Love that will help us our conquest to win, Go tell the world of his love.
Fill'd with his fulness, no longer forbear, Go tell the world of his love.
Love that will bring us to glo-ry at last, Go tell the world of his love.

D.S.—Heirs to the kingdom of Jesus the Lord, Go tell the world of his love.

CHORUS.

D.S.

Go tell the world, Go tell the world, Go tell the world of his love of his love;

C

Home at Last.

FANNY J. CROSBY.

Melody by M LINDSAY.
Arr by W. J. K.

1. Hark the song of ho-ly rap-ture, Hear it break from yonder strand,
2. Oh, the long and sweet re-un-ion, Where the bells of time shall cease,
3. Look beyond, the skies are clear-ing; See, the mist dis-solves a-way;

Where our friends for us are wait-ing, In the gold-en, sum-mer land;
Oh, the greet-ing, endless greet-ing, On the ver-nal heights of peace;
Soon our eyes will catch the dawning Of a bright, ce-les-tial day;

They have reach'd the port of glo-ry, O'er the Jor-dan they have passed,
Where the hop-ing and des-pond-ing Of the wea-ry heart are past,
Soon the shadows will be lift-ed That around us now are cast.

And with mil-,lions they are shout-ing, Home at last, home at last:
And we en-ter life e-ter-nal,—Home at last, home at last:
And re-joic-ing we shall gath-er Home at last, home at last:

And with mil-lions they are shout-ing, Home at last, home at last.
And we en-ter life e-ter-nal,—Home at last, home at last.
And re-joic-ing we shall gath-er Home at last, home at last.

At the Golden Landing.

EDGAR PAGE.

JNO. R. SWENBY.

1. Friends of yore have flown to heaven, Springing from the house of clay;
2. Oft- en at the shades of evening, When I sit me down to rest,
3. And I seem to see their fac- es, Beaming with ce- les- tial love,
4. And I think I hear them speaking, As they oft- en spake to me,
5. Broth- er, sis- ter, faithful sol- dier, If our mingling here so sweet,

Glad to gain their joy - ful free- dom, Borne by an - gel bands a- way.
One by one I count them o - ver, They who are in glo - ry blest.
Shin- ing as their blessed Mas - ter, White-robed, with the saints above.
While I seem to hear them say - ing, "Pil- grim, heaven is waiting thee."
What shall be our joy- ous rap- ture When we at the landing meet!

CHORUS.

While on Pisgah's mount I'm standing, Looking t'ward the vernal shore,

There I seem to see them banding, Just beside the Golden Landing,

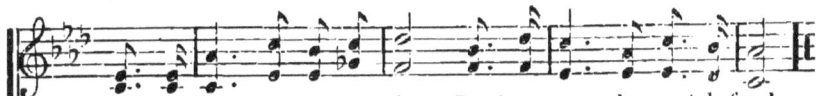

Wait- ing to receive me o'er, Precious ones who went before!

Work, Vote, Pray.

E. E. Hewitt

Wm. J. Kirkpatrick.

1. We will work, we will work for the temperance cause, For the sake of the
2. We will pray, we will pray, for the temperance cause, To our God ev - er
3. We will vote, we will vote for the temperance cause, We will ral - ly our
4. As we work, as we pray, so we mean to vote; Let our watchword ring

land that we love; For the sake of the souls who are tempted to sin,
rul - ing on high; He is might - i - er still than the hosts of the foe,
strength at the polls; We'll remem - ber the wives who are praying at home;
bold - ly again; Here are hearts, here are hands, here are courage and faith,

CHORUS.

We will lift up our ban - ner a-bove.
Though they gather his power to de - fy.
We'll remem - ber the per - il of souls.
And may God give his bless- ing, A - men.

We will work and pray, we will vote al - way For the men who will make better laws: better laws; We will work and pray, we will labor night and day For the good of the temperance cause.

Joy in Heaven.

E. E. HEWITT. Wm. J. KIRKPATRICK.

1. There is joy among the angels, There's a mighty shout of rapture; Far be-
2. There is joy among the angels By the shining, crystal riv - er, For a
3. There is ho - ly joy in heaven Higher, pur - er than the angels'; 'Tis the

yond the pearly gates the news has come Of a sinner now repenting, To the
wand'ring one is safe within the fold; For the Shepherd sought and found him, And the
Father's heart rejoicing in its love; 'Tis the Saviour-Shepherd singing O'er the

gospel-word consenting,—Of a contrite soul that seeks its better home.
arms of love are round him; Hear the music grandly ring from harps of gold.
lost one he is bringing, Bringing to the ev - erlast- ing home a- bove.

CHORUS.

Joy, joy, joy, joy in heaven, Souls are seeking now the living way; There is

Joy, joy, joy, joy among the angels; Join their hallelujah songs to-day. to-day.

38 We shall Walk the Realms of Glory.

EMMA PITT.   WM. J. KIRKPATRICK.

1. We shall walk the realms of glory, Where e - ter - nal beauty reigns,
2. We shall walk the realms of glory With the blood-wash'd, mighty throng,
3. We shall walk the realms of glory, And by Je - sus' side sit down;
4. We shall walk the realms of glory, Where no tears can ev - er come,

There with ser - aph hosts unnumbered Join the grand immor - tal strains.
We shall join the an - gel harpers In their ev - erlast-ing song.
Clad no more in robes of sor- row, We shall wear a fadeless crown.
Where the sun - light is not needed, In that sweet, e - ter - nal home.

CHORUS.

We shall walk the realms of glory, With the loved ones gone be - fore,

rit.

We shall sing the sweet old sto - ry, O - ver on the oth- er shore.

Not Satisfied Here.

Rev. J. Lemacks Stokes. Psa. xvii. 15. L. L. Pickett.

1. I know the joy of pardoned sin, The witness sweet and clear;
2. I know the cleansing from all sin, The freedom from all care;
3. I know the blessed sheltering wings, His guiding hand so dear,

But sat - is - fied I have not been, E'en with that portion fair.
And yet I am not sat - is - fied, Nor can be, brother, here.
And heavenly mu - sic through me rings, But sat - is - fied? Not here.

REFRAIN.

Not sat- isfied here, not sat- isfied here, I am not sat- isfied here;

Not sat- isfied here, not sat- isfied here, I shall be sat- isfied there.

4 I run on duty's errands fleet,
  I feel the Master near,
  But more I long to be complete,
  His perfect likeness bear!

5 No, no, my Lord, not satisfied,
  Till full redemption's given,
  And the free spirit at thy side,
  Shall live the life of heaven.

40

Blessed Light of God.

E. A. BARNES.   *"His marvellous light." 1 Peter. ii. 9.*   JNO. R. SWENEY.

1. Day by day we journey here, In the light of God: Shadows lift and
2. We have gospel words to speak, In the light of God; We have err-ing
3. All our joys so sweetly blend, In the light of God; And our joys will

dis-appear, In the light of God. Here his precepts we obey, Here 'tis
ones to seek, In the light of God. Life its cares and duties bring, Yet 'tis
nev-er end, In the light of God. We have words of love and cheer, And we

sweet to sing and pray, And our hope fades not away, In the light of God.
sweet to work and sing, As its days are on the wing, In the light of God.
never need to fear While in faith we journey here, In the light of God.

CHORUS.

In . . . the light, Blessed light of God, . In the light, in the light,
In the light, . . in the light, Blessed light, - light of God,

Blessed light of God! We all rejoice as we journey home, In the light, in the light, We all rejoice as we journey home, In the blessed light of God.

Father all Holy.

E. E. HEWITT.   THE LORD'S PRAYER.   WM. J. KIRKPATRICK.

1. Father all ho - ly, bend we so lowly, Glowing with love's tender flame,
2. Angels adore thee, waiting before thee, Swift thy commands to fulfil:
3. From sin deliv - er, keep us forev - er, Kingdom and glory are thine,

Father in heaven, praises be giv - en, Hallowed forev - er thy Name.
Grant us, we pray thee, grace to obey thee, Choosing and serving thy will.
Thine, too, the power, hear us this hour, Father, our Father divine!

Telling the story, spreading thy glory, Send forth thy people, we pray,
Father, now lead us, day by day feed us, Ever provide and defend;
Jesus is pleading, still interceding For his redeemed ones again,

Till every nation know thy salvation, Under thy kingdom's full sway.
Trespass confessing, seeking thy blessing, Pardon and peace without end.
For his sake hear us, in his name cheer us, He is the faithful "Amen."

God so Loved the World.

FANNY J. CROSBY.   John iii. 16.   WM. J. KIRKPATRICK.

Solo ad lib.

1. God loved the world so tenderly His only Son he gave, That all who on his
2. Oh, love that only God can feel, And only he can show! Its height and depth, its
3. Why perish, then, ye ransom'd ones? Why slight the gracious call? Why turn from him
4. O Saviour, melt these hearts of ours, And teach us to believe That whosoever [whose

CHORUS.

name believe Its wondrous pow'r will save. For God so loved the world that he
length and breadth Nor heav'n nor earth can know!
words proclaim E-ter-nal life to all?
comes to thee Shall endless life receive.

gave his on-ly Son, That who-so-ev-er be-lieveth in him

Should not per-ish, should not per-ish; That who-so-ev-er be-

lieveth in him Should not per-ish, but have ev-er-last-ing life.

SALLIE L. SMITH.   JNO. R. SWENEY.

1. All   is read-y, the Mas-ter said, All   is read-y, the feast is spread;
2. All   is read-y, he call-eth still; Come, and welcome, whoev-er will;
3. Though his mercy prolongs your day, Time is precious, no more de-lay;
4. Take the pardon his love bestows, Take the water   of life that flows;

Sweet his message of love   to all, Yet how many will slight the call!
Bring your burden of doubts and fears, Bring your sorrow, your cares, and tears.
Now he listens to hear your prayer, Haste the garment of praise to wear.
Lo,   he standeth be-side the door: Hear the Spirit, your hearts implore.

CHORUS.

Why, why, why will ye die? Ask, and the Saviour will free-ly   forgive;

Why, why, why will ye   die? On-ly   a look, and your soul shall live.

44 Leaning on the Everlasting Arms.

Rev. E. A. Hoffman.   A. J. Showalter.

1. What a fel- lowship, what a joy divine, Leaning on the ev - er -
2. Oh, how sweet to walk in this pilgrim way, Leaning on the ev - er -
3. What have I to dread, what have I to fear, Leaning on the ev - er -

last - ing arms; What a bless - ed - ness, What a peace is mine,
last - ing arms; Oh, how bright the path grows from day to day,
last - ing arms? I have bless - ed peace with my Lord so near,

REFRAIN.

Lean - ing on the ev - er - last - ing arms. Lean - ing,
Lean - ing on the ev - er - last - ing arms.
Lean - ing on the ev - er - last - ing arms. Lean - ing on Je - sus,

lean - ing, Safe and se-cure from all a - larms;
Lean - ing on Je - sus,

Lean - ing, lean - ing, Leaning on the ev- er- lasting arms.
Lean-ing on Je - sus, lean- ing on Je - sus,

By per. A. J. Showalter.

Trusting Jesus, That is All.

EDGAR PAGE.   JNO. R. SWENEY.

1. Sim - ply trusting ev - 'ry day; Trusting, though a stormy way;
2. Bright-ly doth his Spir - it shine In - to this poor heart of mine;
3. Sing - ing, if my way is clear; Pray - ing, if the path is drear;
4. Trust- ing as the moments fly, Trust - ing as the days go by,

Ev - en when my faith is small, Trust - ing Je - sus, that is all.
While he leads I can- not fall,— Trust - ing Je - sus, that is all.
If in dan- ger, for him call,— Trust - ing Je - sus, that is all.
Trust- ing him, whate'er be - fall,— Trust - ing Je - sus, that is all.

CHORUS.

Trusting him while life shall last, . Trusting him till earth is past— . .
while life shall last,   till earth is past—

Till within the jas- per wall— . . . . Trusting Jesus, that is all.
the jas - per wall—

The Mind of Jesus.

E. E. HEWITT.　　　　　　　　　　　　　　　　　　　JNO. R. SWENEY.

1. Oh, to have the mind of Je - sus, 　Pur- er than the light of day;
2. Oh, to have the mind of Je - sus, With the heav'nly flame aglow;
3. Oh, to have the mind of Je - sus, On the Father's service bent;
4. Oh, to have the mind of Je - sus, When like him the cross we bear,

Calm as skies that smile at morning, When the storm has passed away!
Scatt'ring love's sweet bene- factions All around us as we go!
Meek and low- ly, true and faithful, With the Father's will content!
Patient in "much tribulation," Joyful through the pow'r of prayer!

CHORUS.

Oh, to have 　the mind of Jesus! Oh, to "see 　him as he

is!" This our highest, holiest longing. This is heaven's crowning bliss.

The Crossings.

Rev. J. L. STOKES. Rev. L. L. PICKETT.

1. Oh, the cru - el E - gypt bondage Of my soul enslaved by sin!
2. Till I heard the voice of Je - sus, Call - ing me to lib - er - ty:
3. So I reached the deep sea- wa- ters, But by faith I soon crossed o'er;
4. Wand'ring, halting, fainting ev - er, Once a - gain my Lord's command
5. Now I rest me in the bowers Of this ho - ly Beulah land,

Oh, the hope- less toil and striving, Foes without and foes within!
"I will lead you, as once Mo- ses Led the peo- ple, through the sea."
Lo! the wil - der- ness of tri - al Lay this side of Canaan's shore.
Called me to the Jor- dan crossing, And I reached the Promised Land.
And am kept from sin and sorrow, 'Neath the sha - dow of his hand.

CHORUS.

Oh, the crossings, Oh, the crossings, From E - gypt to Canaan's shore!

Oh, the crossings, Oh, the crossings! Saviour, lead me safe- ly o'er!

48 I am Weary of Sin.

MARTHA J. LANKTON.   WM. J. KIRKPATRICK.

1. I am wea - ry of sin, and I long to be free, Oh,
2. I am wea - ry of sin, for it lures to de - ceive, On
3. I am wea - ry of sin, and I pray to be thine, To
4. I am wea - ry of sin, of its conflicts and strife, I

say, is there hope for a sinner like me? Can I, who have stray'd o'er the
thee, my Redeemer, I now will believe; I haste as I am to the
lean on thy word, and its promise divine,— To feel in my heart thy pro-
sigh for a pur - er and hap - pi - er life,— A life that is filled with the

dark mountain's brow. Re - turn to the Saviour, and plead with him now?
clear, flowing tide, Where, deep in its bos - om, the past thou wilt hide.
tection and care, And know 'tis thy yoke and thy burden I bear.
fulness of love, Pre - par - ing my spir - it for mansions a - bove.

CHORUS.

I long to be free, I long to be free; O blessed Re-
Till whiter than snow, Till whiter than snow, I'll bathe in its

deemer, have pit - y on me; The fountain lies o - pen, and
waters till whiter than snow; The fountain lies o - pen, and

Copyright, 1890, by Wm. J. Kirkpatrick.

there will I go, And bathe in its waters till whiter than snow.

Hold On, My Soul.

Wm. H. Jones.

Jno. R. Sweney.

1. Hold on, my soul, to the end hold out, With a faith no storm can shock;
2. Hold on, my soul, tho' the light-nings flash, And thy sails all torn may be,
3. Hold on, my soul, tho' the waves run high, For the night and storm shall cease,
4. Hold on, my soul, for the end draws near, And thy voyage is well nigh o'er,

Fine.

Stand firm, stand fast, for the Lord has said He will hide thee in the rifted rock.
For thy hope still points to the polar star, Brightly shining thro' the clouds for thee.
There is light beyond,'tis the morning breaks, Thou art coming to the port of peace.
And the welcome-home thou hast longed to hear Soon will greet thee on the golden
shore.

D.S.—on, my soul, for the Lord has said He will hide thee in the rifted rock

CHORUS.

D.S.

Hold on, (hold on,) hold on, (hold on,) With a faith no storm can shock, Hold

50

Tell it to Jesus.

J. E. RANKIN, D. D.   Matt. xiv. 12.   E. S. LORENZ. By per.

1. Are you wea - ry, are you heavy - hearted? Tell it to Je - sus,
2. Do the tears flow down your cheeks un- bidden? Tell it to Je - sus,
3. Do you fear the gath'ring clouds of sorrow? Tell it to Je - sus,
4. Are you troubled at the thought of dying? Tell it to Je - sus,

Tell it to Je - sus; Are you grieving o - ver joys de - part - ed?
Tell it to Je - sus; Have you sins that to man's eye are hidden?
Tell it to Je - sus; Are you anxious what shall be to - mor - row?
Tell it to Je - sus; For Christ's coming Kingdom are you sigh - ing?

CHORUS.

Tell it to Je - sus a - lone. Tell it to Je-sus, tell it to Je-sus,

He is a friend that's well known; You have no oth - er

such a friend or broth - er, Tell it to Je - sus a - lone.

Mrs. R. N. Turner. Wm. J Kirkpatrick.

1. O, why dost thou linger so long Out- side in the danger and cold?
2. The light streameth out from the door, Behold it and en- ter and live!
3. Who comes to the fold of my care Shall drink from the fountain of joy,
4. Then come without waiting or doubt, Bring all of your burdens to me;

Come home to the shel- ter and warmth, Come home to the joy of the fold.
The ser- vice of love is most sweet; And life ev- erlast- ing I give.
And works of de - vo- tion and love His heart and his hands shall employ.
There's rest in the shelter of home, There's rest and there's comfort for thee.

CHORUS.

Come home, come home, I am calling to-day; Come home, I am waiting for thee:

am waiting for thee;

Come home, come home, to the arms of my love, I am waiting, waiting for thee.

of my love, I am waiting, waiting for thee.

Redeemed, Praise the Lord.

ABBIE MILLS.   WM. J. KIRKPATRICK.

1. O happy day! what a Sav-iour is mine! I am redeemed, praise the Lord!
2. O clap your hands, all ye people of God, I am redeemed, praise the Lord!
3. Thanks be to God for the great vict'ry given, I am redeemed, praise the Lord!
4. Glory to God, I would shout ev - ermore, I am redeemed, praise the Lord!

Fine.

All to his pleasure I glad-ly re-sign, I am redeemed, praise the Lord!
Let ev'ry tongue speak his mercy abroad, I am redeemed, praise the Lord!
Now I am free; ev'ry chain has been riven,—I am redeemed, praise the Lord!
O for a voice that could reach ev'ry shore, I am redeemed, praise the Lord!

Key C.

Jesus has taken my burden away; Jesus has turned all my night into day;
His loving-kindness is better than gold; He doth bestow more than my cup can hold;
Out of the pit, and the mire, and the clay, Jesus has borne me in triumph away;
Help me, ye ransom'd, awake, ev'ry string, Let earth rejoice and the whole heavens ring,

Use first four lines as Chorus. D. C.

Jesus has come to my heart,—come to stay,—I am redeemed, praise the Lord!
Wondrous Salvation, that ne'er can be told,—I am redeemed, praise the Lord!
Safe on the rock I am standing to-day,—I am redeemed, praise the Lord!
While we the chorus u - ni - ted-ly sing, I am redeemed, praise the Lord!

Mrs. C. N. Pickop. Wm. J. Kirkpatrick.

1. Come to Je - sus, trembling sin - ner, With your load of guilt oppressed;
2. He is waiting, he is read - y, Ten - der, lov - ing words to say;
3. Time is fly - ing, do not tar - ry, Haste, while it is called to - day!
4. Do not lin - ger, do not tri - fle, Heed your loving Saviour's call;

Come to Je - sus, he will save you, Come, and he will give you rest.
Will you not ac - cept his bless - ing? Give your heart to him to - day?
Can you spurn his ten - der plead - ing? Can you turn this friend a - way?
In his ten - der heart there's mer - cy, In his arms there's room for all.

CHORUS.

Come to Je - - - sus, come to Je - - - sus, Wea - ry
Come, oh, come to - day, come, oh, come to - day,

sinner, come to Jesus while you may; He will save you, he will
He will save to - day,

save you, Wea - ry sinner, he will save you, come to - day. come to-day.
he will save to - day,

54   The Saviour is My All in All.

P. B.   "Wherefore he is able to save them to the uttermost."—Heb. vii. 25.   P. Bilhorn.

1. The Saviour is my all in all, He is my constant theme!
2. His Spir-it gives sweet peace within, And bids all care de - part!
3. And whatso - ev - er I may ask, To glo - ri - fy his name,
4. Oh, praise the Lord, my soul, rejoice, Give thanks unto thy God!

rit.

By sim - ply trusting in his word He keeps me pure and clean.
He fills my soul with righteousness, And pu - ri - fies the heart.
The Fa - ther free - ly gives to me, Since Christ the Saviour came.
Who took thee in thy sin - fulness, And cleansed thee by his blood!

CHORUS.

Glo - ry! oh, glo - ry! Je - sus hath redeemed me;

rit.

Glo - ry! oh, glo - ry! He washed my sins a - way, a - way!

Free Waters.

Mrs. M. B. C. Sladn.

Dr. A. B. Everett. By per.

1. There's a fountain free, 'tis for you and me: Let us haste, oh, haste to its brink;
2. There's a living stream, with a crystal gleam: From the throne of life now it flows;
3. There's a living well and its waters swell, And e-ter-nal life they can give;
4. There's a rock that's cleft and no soul is left, That may not its pure waters share;

'Tis the fount of love from the Source above, And he bids us all freely drink.
While the wa-ters roll let the weary soul Hear the call that forth freely goes.
And we joyful sing, ever spring, oh, spring, As we haste to drink and to live.
'Tis for you and me, and its stream I see: Let us hasten joy-ful-ly there.

CHORUS.

Will you come to the fountain free? Will you come? 'tis for you and me;

Will you come,

Will you come,

Thirsty soul, hear the welcome call : 'Tis a fountain open'd for all.

Thirsty soul,

Jesus is Calling for Thee.

LIDIE H. EDMUNDS.   REV. L. L. PICKETT.

1. O come, to Cal-va-ry turning, Je-sus is calling for thee; His heart so
2. O hark! in life's sunny morning, Jesus is calling for thee; Sweet flowers thy
3. O soul so burdened and weary, Jesus is calling for thee; He'll lift the
4. But still the Saviour is calling, Jesus is calling for thee; Though now the

tenderly yearning, Jesus is calling for thee. Come now, and enter the
pathway adorning, Jesus is calling for thee. He sends thee gladness and
shadows so dreary, Jesus is calling for thee. In love thy troubles are
night-dews are falling, Jesus is calling for thee. E'en though so long thou hast

fountain, Fountain of mercy so free; Though sin arise like a mountain,
pleasure, Wilt thou not thank him to-day? Come now, and seek endless treasure,
giv-en, Sorrow is on-ly his voice That bids thee look up to Heaven,
slighted, Slighted salvation so great, Yet his own promise is plighted,

CHORUS.

Je-sus is call-ing for thee.   Call-ing, call-ing, Je-sus is
Joys that are brighter than day.
Look, and in Je-sus re-joice.
Come; Je-sus stands at the gate.

calling for thee,   Call-ing, call-ing, Je-sus is call-ing for thee.

Purity, Whiter than Snow,

Rev. John O. Foster.　　　　　　　　　　　　Jno. R. Sweney.

1. In - to the fountain of cleansing we go, Down where the waters of
2. Oh, what a won - der- ful pow- er is there, Sav- ing the soul from its
3. Here, by this Fount of Sal - va- tion we stay, O - pen for sin and un-
4. Christ has revealed his deep love to my soul, Now by his mer-its my

pur - i - ty flow, Troubled to - day is that Fountain we know,
ut - ter de - spair, Wash-ing and cleansing we all now may share.
clean-ness to - day, Guilt and cor- rup- tion are ban- ished a - way,—
heart is made whole, Wide are the waves of his ful - ness that roll;

D.S.—Come where the waters of pur - i - ty flow,

Fine.　　　　REFRAIN.

Wash- ing us whit - er than snow.　　Whit - - - - er than
Pur - i - ty, whit - er than snow!
Pur - i - ty, whit - er than snow.
Pur - i - ty, whit - er than snow.　　Whit - er than snow,

Wash and be whit - er than snow.

D.S.

snow, ... Whit - - - - er than snow, ...
whit - er than snow, Whit - er than snow, whit - er than snow,

There's a Beautiful Land.

JAMES NICHOLSON.   WM. U. BUTCHER.

1. There's a beauti- ful land on   high,   To its glories I fain would fly,—
2. There's a beauti- ful land on   high,   I shall en - ter it by and by,
3. There's a beauti- ful land on   high,   Then why should I fear to   die,
4. There's a beauti- ful land on   high,   And my kindred its bliss en - joy,

When by sorrows press'd down, I long for my crown, In that beautiful land on high.
There, with friends hand in hand, I shall walk on the strand, In that beautiful, etc.
When death is the way to the realms of day, In that beautiful land on high.
Methinks I now see how they're waiting for me, In that beautiful land on high.

REFRAIN.

In that beauti- ful land I'll   be,   From earth and its cares set   free;

My Je - sus is there, he's gone to prepare, A place in that land for   me.

5 There's a beautiful land on high;
  And though here I oft weep and sigh,
My Jesus hath said that no tears shall be [shed
  In that beautiful land on high.

6 There's a beautiful land on high,
  Where we never shall say, "good-bye!"
When over the river we are happy forever,
  In that beautiful land on high.

Gather the Reapers Home.

JENNIE JOHNSON.

JNO. R. SWENEY.

1. Have ye heard the song from the golden land ? Have ye heard the glad new song,
2. They are looking down from the golden land, Our beloved are looking down,
3. O the song rolls on from the golden land, And our hearts are strong to-day,
4. O the song rolls on from the golden land, From its vales of joy and flowers,

Let us bind our sheaves with a willing hand, For the time will not be long.
They have done their work, they have borne their cross,
            And received their promised crown.
For it nerves our souls with its music sweet, And we toil in the noon-tide ray.
And we feel and know by a liv- ing faith That its tones will soon be ours

REFRAIN.

The Lord of the harvest will soon appear, His smile, his voice we shall see and hear,

The Lord of the harvest will soon appear   And gather the reapers home.

60

Meet me There.

Henrietta E. Blair.   Wm. J. Kirkpatrick.

1. On the happy, golden shore, Where the faithful part no more, When the
2. Here our fondest hopes are vain, Dearest links are rent in twain; But in
3. Where the harps of angels ring, And the blest for-ev - er sing, In the

storms of life are o'er, Meet me there; Where the night dissolves away Into
heav'n no throb of pain, Meet me there; By the river sparkling bright, In the
palace of the King, Meet me there; Where in sweet communion blend Heart with

Fine.

pure and perfect day. I am going home to stay, Meet me there.
ci - ty of delight, Where our faith is lost in sight, Meet me there.
heart, and friend with friend, In a world that ne'er shall end, Meet me there.

D.S.—happy golden shore, Where the faithful part no more, Meet me there.

CHORUS.

Meet me there,   Meet me there,   Where the tree of life is

D.S.

blooming, Meet me there;   When the storms of life are o'er, On the

Meet me there;

To Save a Poor Sinner.

Rev. John O. Foster, A. M.

Grace I. Foster.

1. I'll sing of the story, how Jesus from glory Has saved a poor
2. His glory immortal bright over the portal, Has banished the
3. Tho' seasons of error, and moments of terror, Like billows of
4. My peace like a river flows onward forever, A tide to e-

sinner like me; That all who believe him, and all who receive him, His
gloom from the grave; The Lord has ascended, the darkness is ended, And
sorrow may roll; In Christ I'm confiding, in him I am hiding, With
terni-ty's sea; To swell the old story with voices in glory, He

CHORUS.

blessed salvation may see. Then sing the glad chorus, His
now he is mighty to save.
safe-ty and rest to my soul.
saved a poor sinner like me.

banner is o'er us, His mercy is boundless and free, From heaven de-

rit.

scended, His love is extended, To save a poor sinner like me.

The Lights of Home.

PRISCILLA J. OWENS   WM. J. KIRKPATRICK.

Question in italics responses in roman type.

1. *Steersman, steersman, the channel's rough and dark, The waves roll high, the*
2. *Steersman, steersman, the stars are wrapped in mist.* The Pol-ar star still
3. *Steersman, steersman, how wild the tempest raves!* The floods may swell, but

winds sweep by, Now whither speeds thy bark? Now whither speeds thy bark!
beams a - far On hills of am - e - thyst, On hills of am - e - thyst.
all is well, While Jesus walks the waves, While Jesus walks the waves.

Sail - ing, sail - ing, to reach a glorious home, Tho' storms assail we
Sail - ing, sail - ing, to find a bet-ter land, No wind that blows our
Sail - ing, sail - ing, to find a happier shore, A pathway bright shines

CHORUS.

dare the gale, For Je - sus bids us come. Sail - - ing o'er the
hope o'erthrows, While Christ waits on the strand.
through the night, Where friends have gone before. Sail - ing, sail - ing,

rest - less tide, Sail - - - ing thro' the gale we glide,
Sail - ing, sail - ing

rit.

There, . . . beyond the billows' foam, We see the lights of home.

There, be - yond, beyond

Battling for the Lord.

T. E. PERKINS.

SEMI-CHORUS.   **CHORUS.**   **SEMI-CHORUS.**

1. We've 'list-ed in a ho - ly war, Battling for the Lord! E - ter-nal
2. We've girded on our armor bright, Battling for the Lord! Our Captain's
3. We'll stand like heroes on the field, Battling for the Lord! And no - bly

CHORUS.   **FULL CHORUS.**

life, our guiding star, Battling for the Lord! We'll work till Jesus comes,
word our strength and might, Battling for the Lord!
fight, but never yield, Battling for the Lord!

We'll work till Je - sus comes, We'll work till Je - sus comes, And

then we'll rest at home.

4 Though sin and death our way oppose,
   Battling for the Lord!
   Through grace we'll conquer all our foes,
   Battling for the Lord!

5 And when our glorious war is o'er,
   Battling for the Lord!
   We'll shout salvation evermore,
   Battling for the Lord!

In the Book of Life.

LIZZIE EDWARDS.　　　　　　　　　　　　　　　　　WM. J. KIRKPATRICK.

1. In   thy book, where glory bright Shines with never - fad - ing light,
2. In   the book, whose pages tell Who have tried to serve thee well,
3. In   the book, where thou dost keep Record still of years that sleep,
4. O   my Saviour, thou canst show What I long so much to know:

Where thy saved thou wilt re - cord, Write my name, my name, O Lord.
O'er my name let mer - cy trace Child of God, redeemed by grace.
Let my name be writ - ten down Heir to life's im - mor - tal crown.
Let my faith be - hold and see That my life is hid with thee.

CHORUS.

Write my name in the book of life, Lamb of God, write it there;

Where thy saved thou wilt re - cord Write my name, my name, O Lord.

Rev. L. L. Pickett. By per.

1. Oh, when shall I dwell in a man - sion all bright, And
2. No pearl from the o - cean or gold from the mine, Can
3. But, while I'm a stran - ger, a - way from my home, I'll

Je - sus, my Sa - viour, be - hold? Or walk by his side, like an
par - don or pu - ri - ty buy: I'll trust in the blood of a
toil in the vine - yard and pray: I'll car - ry the cross, while I

an - gel of light, In a cit - y all garnished with gold.
Sa - viour di - vine, And cling to the cross till I die.
think of the crown, And watch for the break of the day.

CHORUS.

Home of the blest! Home of the blest! When wilt thou ev - er be mine?

Home of the blest! Home of the blest! Soon shalt thou ev - er be mine.

I Come to Thee.

E. E. Hewitt.

Wm. J. Kirkpatrick.

1. From yonder cross what beams divine Of peace, and hope, and mercy shine,
2. Thy kind, in-vit-ing voice I know; Thy wounded hands new life bestow:
3. As seeks the wear-y bird its nest When sunset lin-gers in the west,

Oh, be each bless-ed promise mine; I come, dear Lord, to thee.
Those hands will nev-er let me go; I come, dear Lord, to thee.
So now, for pardon, healing, rest, I come, dear Lord, to thee.

CHORUS.

I come to thee, I come to thee; Thine out-stretched arms I see;

I come to thee, I come to thee, Dear Lord, who died for me.

4 'Midst pressing care and daily need
Thy overruling love I read,
For help, thy "present help," I plead;
I come, dear Lord, to thee.

5 In weakness be my mighty Tower,
My Refuge in temptation's hour;
My brightest joy when blessings
I come, dear Lord, to thee. [shower;

Speak to Me, Jesus.

H. L. G.   H. L. Gilmour.

1. Speak to me, Je - sus, I'm far from thy fold; Far from kind friends, that so
2. Speak to me, Je - sus, in tones that so oft, in sickness and sorrow, so
3. Speak to me, Je - sus, oh, tell of thy power, Mighty to save, when my
4. Speak to me, Je - sus, thy Spir - it im - part, To strengthen, to comfort, and

oft - en have told That sto - ry so simple, so kind and so free, Oh,
ten- der and soft, Did gently ad - monish in Beth - a- ny's home, Oh,
wand'rings are o'er; I seek now for pardon, in pen - i- tence wait, Oh,
cheer my weak heart; Thy voice I have heard, and thy blood is applied; Oh,

D. S.—get not thy blood, that from sin makes so free; Oh,

Fine.   CHORUS.

speak to me, Je - sus, I'll lis - ten to thee.   Speak . . to me
speak to me, Je - sus, to thee I will come,
speak to me, Je - sus, be - fore 'tis too late.   Speak to me, speak to me,
help me, dear Saviour to live at thy side.

speak to me, Je - sus, I will come to thee.
(3d verse.)—I now come to thee.
(4th verse.)—I have come to thee.

Je - sus, speak . . from a - bove,   Tell . . . of thy
speak to me, speak from a - bove   Tell of thy hands,

P

D. S.

hands, . . . of thy side, . . . and thy love; . . . For-
tell of thy side,   tell of thy hands, of thy side, and thy love;

Copyright, 1881, by John J. Hood.

Come Over.

F. A. B.

F. A. BLACKMER.

1. Come o-ver, lost one, come O-ver the line to-day, Where Je-sus
2. On-ly a step to God, One step to cross the line; Hast-en, O
3. Moment of priceless worth, When God has drawn so near; His wondrous
4. Dare not this call refuse, When du-ty is so plain; The Spir-it
5. Lost one, this call to you May be the ver-y last! Haste! ere for-

CHORUS.

bids you stand; Oh, come a-way. Come o-ver, oh, come o-ver, Come
dy-ing one, Touch the Divine!
ten-der-ness, Sin-ner, re-vere.
long denied Comes not a-gain.
ev-er-more Your day be past.

over the line to-day; And heav'n delight, while men invite, And angels seem to

say, Come o-ver, oh, come o-ver, Come o-ver the line to-day;

rit.

To Je-sus bow, He calls you now, Come over the line to-day.

Entire Consecration.

FRANCES RIDLEY HAVERGAL.   Chorus by W. J. K.   WM. J. KIRKPATRICK.

1. Take my life, and let it be   Con - se - crat - ed, Lord, to thee;
2. Take my feet, and let them be   Swift and beau - ti - ful for thee;
3. Take my lips, and let them be   Filled with mes - sag - es for thee;
4. Take my moments and my days,   Let them flow in endless praise;

Take my hands and let them move   At the impulse of thy love.
Take my voice and let me sing   Al - ways, on - ly, for my King.
Take my sil - ver and my gold,—   Not a mite would I withhold.
Take my in - tel - lect, and use   Ev - 'ry power as thou shalt choose.

CHORUS.

{ Wash me in the Saviour's precious blood, the precious blood,
{ Cleanse me in its pu - ri - fy - ing flood, the healing flood, } Lord, I give to

thee, my life and all, to be, Thine, henceforth, e - ter - nal - ly.

5 Take my will, and make it thine;
   It shall be no longer mine;
   Take my heart.—it is thine own,—
   It shall be thy royal throne.

6 Take my love,—my Lord, I pour
   At thy feet its treasure-store!
   Take myself, and I will be
   Ever, only, all for thee!

Walking and Talking.

SALLIE SMITH.

JNO. R. SWENEY.

1. I am saved thro' the blood of my cru - ci - fied Lord, With his
2. I am saved thro' the blood of my cru - ci - fied Lord, And the
3. Tho' the tempt - er as - sail, yet he can - not pre - vail, I am
4. Thro' his won - der - ful love, my Re - deem - er a - bove, Is pre-

chil - dren my lot I have cast; I will lift up my voice, I will
glo - ry to him will I give; For the grace he bestows and his
un - der my Saviour's con - trol, And the more I be - lieve still the
par - ing a man - sion for me, Where from toil I shall rest with the

sing and re - joice That from death un - to life I have passed.
good - ness that flows, I will praise him as long as I live.
more I re - ceive Of his full - ness of joy in my soul.
hap - py and blest, And for - ev - er his face I shall see.

REFRAIN.

I am walk - ing, I am talk - ing, with my Lord and King In the

shad - ow of the cross all the day, all the day, I am walking, I am

Sweet Day of the Lord.

Mrs. R. N. Turner

J. H. Kurzenknabe.

1. Sweet day of the Lord, we hail thee with joy, We welcome thee gladly once more;
2. Oh, bright is the hour when spent in his house, And precious the moments of peace;
3. The Lord in his house a - bid - eth to-day, His Spirit gives comfort to all;
4. Sweet day of the Lord, sweet Sabbath on earth, Thy hours of refreshment we love;

A - bove all the cares and la - bors of life, Our songs of devotion shall soar.
The flame of our hearts shall kindle a- new, And love and devotion increase.
Then come, ask for mer- cy, pardon, and grace, Give heed to his sweet, loving call.
Our songs shall ascend in rapture and praise, And soar in their fulness above.

REFRAIN.

Up to the presence of In - fi-nite Love, We rise in our worship to - day;

Ask- ing his blessing, his blessing divine, We joy - ful-ly bear it a- way.

Glorious as the Light.

L. W. Smith.

"And they shall be mine, saith the Lord of hosts, in that day when I make up my jewels."—Mal iii: 17.

F. A. Blackmer.

1. When the jewels of earth shall be gather'd, They with glory effulgent shall shine,
2. What a host there will be of the sav'd ones! Like the stars of the night, we are told,
3. They are those who have follow'd the Saviour, Out of ev - er - y nation and tribe,
4. "Thou art worthy, O Christ," they are singing,
"Who hath died, all our race to redeem."

As they come to the gates of that city, Sweeping in thro' its portals divine.
As they march in their strength and their grandeur,
Thro' the bright, shining streets of pure gold.
Who have come thro' a great tribulation, Praises loud they to Jesus ascribe.
"Hallelujah!" the grand swelling chorus, And his love everlasting their theme.

CHORUS.

Glo - rious as the light of the king - - - - dom! Glorious as the
Glo - ri - ous as the light,

bright, ris - ing sun.
as the bright, ris - ing sun.
Oh, what a rapt'rous sight, In that

heav'nly home so bright,—As glo- rious as the light of the kingdom!

Stepping=stones to Jesus.

E. E. Hewitt.
Wm J. Kirkpatrick.

Moderato.

1. Stepping-stones to Je-sus All our joys may be, Used with glad thanksgiving
2. Stepping-stones to Je-sus, Leading to his feet, Are the lit-tle tri-als,
3. Stepping-stones to Je-sus, All the pure delight In his works of beauty,
4. Stepping-stones to Jesus, Blessed means of grace; Prayer and sweet communion

For his love so free. Many, many blessings In our pathway fall, Stepping-stones to
Which we daily meet; Ev'ry need that presses, Ev'ry vexing care. Ev'ry dis-ap-
All things fair and bright. Ev'ry sweet affection, Tender human love Brought in conse-
In the sacred place; Ev'ry self-denial For the Master's cause. Each renewed o-

CHORUS.

Jesus We may find them all. Looking for the stepping-stones
pointment, Ev'ry cross we bear.   Placed along life's way;
cration To the Friend above.
beying Of his ho-ly laws.

Looking for the stepping-stones, We find them ev'ry day; Stepping-stones to Jesus,

p   *poco rit.*   *ad lib.*

Stepping-stones to Jesus, Looking for the stepping-stones, We find them ev'ry day.

74 Gathered Home.

SELECTED.

CHAS. EDW. POLLOCK.

1. Shall we all meet at home in the morn - ing, On the shores of the
2. Shall we all meet at home in the morn - ing, And from sor - row for -
3. Shall we all meet at home in the morn - ing, There our bless-ed Re -

bright, crystal sea, With the loved ones who long have been waiting? What a
ev - er be free? Shall we join in the songs of the ransomed? What a
deem - er to see? Shall we know and be known by our loved ones? What a

REFRAIN.

meet - ing, in-deed, that will be! Gath-ered home, Gathered
meet - ing, in-deed, that will be! Gath-ered home,
meet - ing, in-deed, that will be!

home. On the shores of the bright, crystal sea;
Gath-ered home, crys - tal sea;

Gathered home, Gathered home, With the loved ones forever to be.
Gathered home, Gathered home,

Keep me ever Close to Thee.

FANNY J. CROSBY. WM. J. KIRKPATRICK.

1. Source from whence the streams of mercy Like a riv-er flow to me,
2. There my life, my hope and com-fort, There a ref-uge for my soul
3. There, in ho-ly, sweet com-munion With thy Spir-it day by day,
4. Close to thee, O Saviour, keep me, Till I reach the shining shore,—

With thy cords of love so ten-der Bind and keep me close to thee.
When the clouds hang darkly round me, And the dis-tant surg-es roll.
Faith to realms of light and glo-ry Bears my raptured soul a-way.
Till I join the raptured arm-y, Shouting joy for ev-er-more.

REFRAIN.

Keep me ev-er close to thee, Blessed Saviour, dear to me, With thy

cords of love so tender Bind and keep me close to thee; Keep me ever close to

thee, Blessed Saviour, dear to me, Bind and keep me close to thee.

Sing On.

Carrie M. Wilson.   Jno. R. Sweney.

1. Sing on, ye joy-ful pil-grims, Nor think the moments long;
2. Sing on, ye joy-ful pil-grims, While here on earth we stay
3. Sing on, ye joy-ful pil-grims, The time will not be long

My faith is heav'nward ris - ing With ev - 'ry tune-ful song;
Let songs of home and Je - sus Be - guile each fleet-ing day;
Till in our Fa-ther's king - dom We swell a no - bler song,

Lo! on the mount of bless - ing, The glo-rious mount! I stand,
Sing on the grand old sto - ry Of his re-deem-ing love,—
Where those we love are wait - ing To greet us on the shore,

And, look-ing o - ver Jor - dan, I see the promised land.
The ev - er-last-ing cho - rus That fills the realms a - bove.
We'll meet be-yond the riv - er, Where surg - es roll no more.

CHORUS.

Sing on; oh, bliss-ful mu - sic! With ev - 'ry note you raise

My heart is filled with rap-ture, My soul is lost in praise:

Sing on; oh, bliss-ful mu - sic! With ev - 'ry note you raise

Sing on; bliss - ful, bliss - ful mu - sic,

My heart is filled with rap - ture, My soul is lost in praise.

Up and Onward.

SALLIE MARTIN.   WM. J. KIRKPATRICK.

1. Up for Je - sus! up and onward! Hear him say- ing, "follow me ;"
2. Up for Je - sus! up and onward! In the ear - ly morning bright,
3. Up for Je - sus! up and onward! Through the conflict firmly stand ;
4. Up for Je - sus! up and onward! He will guide us with his eye;

In the no - ble christian arm - y Faithful sol - diers let us be.
With the watchword on our ban - ner, Brave defend - ers of the right.
For we can - not lose a bat - tle With our lead - er in command.
He has promised if we trust him, We shall con - quer by and by.

CHORUS.

Marching on with singing, Sweetest music bringing Unto him that shall reign;

Let the world before us Hear the joyful chorus, Hal- le - lu - jah, a - men.

No Shade like this for Me.

Rev. Horatius Bonar.   D. E. Dortch.

1. Oppress'd with noonday's searching heat, To yon-der cross I flee;
2. Be-neath that cross clear wa-ters burst, A fount-ain sparkling free;
3. A stran-ger here I pitch my tent, Be-neath this spreading tree;
4. For bur-dened ones a rest-ing place Be-side that cross I see;

Be-neath its shel-ter take my seat, No shade like this for me.
And there I quench my des-ert thirst, No spring like this for me.
Here shall my pil-grim life be spent, No home like this for me.
I here cast off my wea-ri-ness, No rest like this for me.

REFRAIN.

No shade like this for me, No shade like this for me;
No spring like this for me, No spring like this for me;
No home like this for me, No home like this for me;
No rest like this for me, No rest like this for me;

Be-neath its shel-ter take my seat, No shade like this for me.
And there I quench my des-ert thirst, No spring like this for me.
Here shall my pil-grim life be spent, No home like this for me.
I here cast off my wea-ri-ness, No rest like this for me.

From "Grace and Glory," by per.

Thine Forever.

FANNY J. CROSBY.   WM. J. KIRKPATRICK.

1. Thine for-ev-er, thine for-ev-er, My Redeem-er, will I be;
2. Thine for-ev-er, thine for-ev-er,—Oh, the rapture of my heart!
3. Where thou leadest I will follow, Where thou bidst me I will go;

On the al-tar lies my offering, Con-se-crated now to thee;
Thou my refuge and my comfort, Thou my lasting portion art;
In the ve-ry front of battle Fear-less will I meet the foe;

All my fervent soul's de-vo-tion To thy service, Lord, I give;
Cast-ing ev-'ry weight behind me, I the christian race will run,
I shall conquer through thy mercy, I shall triumph through thy might,

For thy honor and thy glo-ry I will la-bor while I live.
Trust-ing thee and taking courage, Till the race my soul has won.
I shall see thee in thy kingdom; There will faith be lost in sight.

CHORUS.   p

Thine forev-er, thine for-ev-er, Saviour, I am resting in thy love:
in thy love;

Thine forev - er, thine forev - er, Saviour, I am resting sweetly in thy love.

Will You Come?

PRISCILLA J. OWENS.

WM. J. KIRKPATRICK.

1. Hear the ear - nest in - vi - ta - tion, Wand'rer from the path of right,
2. Christian souls are fervent pray - ing, Ho - ly Spir - it, send thy light,
3. Angels near us, eag - er bending, Friends beloved from homes of light,
4. Hear the Saviour in - ter - ced - ing, Nor his gracious mes - sage slight;

Je - sus of - fers his sal - va - tion; Will you come to Christ to - night?
Why a - far in darkness stray - ing? Why not come to Christ to - night?
With our hearts their question blending, Will you come to Christ to - night?
Will you pass his cross un - heed - ing? Oh, re - turn to Christ to - night.

CHORUS.

Will you come? will you come? Come and at his al - tar bow;

Will you come? will you come? Jesus waits to save you now.

I Will Trust in My Saviour.

Mrs. Loula K. Rogers.

R. M. McIntosh. By per.

1. Tho' the shadows gather o'er my pathway here, And no sun comes with joyous ray,
2. In the tempest when the winds around me roll, And the thunders my heart affright,
3. When the chilling blight of death is on my brow, And the earth passes from my view,

In the darkness not an e - vil will I fear, For my Saviour is leading the way.
Sweetly comes a loving whisper to my soul, Then the world is all beauty and light.
Simply trusting in my Saviour then, as now, He will lead me in paths ever new.

REFRAIN.

I will trust in my Saviour, I will trust in my Saviour, I will

trust in my Saviour al - way; He will lead me thro' the night, By his

ev - er shin-ing light, I will trust in my Sav-iour to - day!

Come and Ask Jesus to Save You.

ABBIE MILLS. WM. J. KIRKPATRICK.

1. { Would you find the way to heaven? Come and ask Jesus to save you; }
{ Would you know your sins forgiven? Come and ask Jesus to save you. }

2. { Would you treasures have a-bove? Come and ask Jesus to save you; }
{ Would you know the wealth of love? Come and ask Jesus to save you. }

He will light and joy im-part To your dark and wea - ry heart,
Come, your lov-ing Fa - ther meet; See, he waits his child to greet;

He will bid your sin de-part, Come and ask Je - sus to save you.
Hast - en on with eag - er feet; Come and ask Je - sus to save you.

CHORUS.

Come to the fountain of mercy to-day, Come and your sins shall be taken away;

Come to the Saviour and earnest - ly pray, Jesus will certainly save you.

3 Would you from your chains be free?
  Come and ask Jesus to save you;
Would you cease a slave to be?
  Come and ask Jesus to save you.
He is every captive's friend;
If on him you now depend,
His right arm will you defend,
  Come and ask Jesus to save you.

4 Would you gain yon heavenly shore?
  Come and ask Jesus to save you;
Would you join those gone before?
  Come and ask Jesus to save you.
He that lives who once was dead
Bore the cross; for you he bled;
He can soothe your dying bed,
  Come and ask Jesus to save you.

The Glory Land.

Mrs. Loula K. Rogers.   R. M. McIntosh. By per.

1. There's a land of love shin-ing far a-bove, In the
2. Oh, I love to sing of the hearts that cling To the
3. And I love to dream of the crys-tal gleam Rest-ing
4. There shall be no night! oh! the bless-ed light That il-

en 1 - less glo - ry of day, And I long to know all the
light of that gold - en shore, Star - ry crowns they'll wear and its
on the bright riv - er there, Of the white-robed throng and the
lumes the heav - en - ly shore! No more sor - row there, and no

REFRAIN.

good who go To that ra - diant land far a - way. Oh, the
glo - ries share With the hap - py ones gone be - fore.
glad new song, And the fade - less flow - ers so fair.
cross to bear; All is joy and peace ev - er more.

glo - ries there are so bright and fair, Here no longer would I roam ; How my

spir - it sighs for the cloudless skies, Of that hap - py, heav - en - ly home.

Glory, I'm Redeemed.

F. A. B.

F. A. BLACKMER.

1. On the Saviour I've believed, Gracious pardon I've received, And his
2. When I heard his loving voice, How it made my heart rejoice, Like sweet
3. All a-long my pil-grim way I will trust him and o-bey, And each
4. Wondrous comfort does he send, Proving such a constant friend, For he

blood now covers all my guilt and shame ; In my soul to dwell he deigns, Without
music to my longing soul it came ; Oh, how wondrous, full and free, Was his
day I'll seek to spread my Saviour's fame ; To ex-alt, my aim shall be, Him who
comes to bless in ev'ry need the same ; Empty turns me not a-way, But new

ri-val there he reigns, Glo-ry, glo-ry, hal-le-lu-jah to his name!
pard'ning love to me! Glo-ry, glo-ry, hal-le-lu-jah to his name!
did so much for me, Glo-ry, glo-ry, hal-le-lu-jah to his name!
blessings sends each day, Glo-ry, glo-ry, hal-le-lu-jah to his name!

CHORUS.

I'm redeemed, I'm redeemed, In his power the Saviour came, And from sin gave

I'm redeemed,   I'm redeemed,   hallelujah,   sweet re-

lease, Filled my soul with heav'nly peace, Glory, glory, hallelujah to his name!

Fire Away with Your Ballots.

Rev. John O. Foster, A.M.   Jno. R. Sweney.

1. You need not wait a - ny long- er For the temp'rance bugle to blow,
2. The Judges made their decision, For the laws are wholesome and strong;
3. March on and go for a lev - y, Break up the hor - ri - ble crime;

The call is loud- er and stronger, You'll hear the trumpet I know.
No long- er an - y di - vi - sion, For li - quor selling · is wrong.
Give law and gos - pel heav - y, A dou - ble barr'l at a time.

The long deep roll has been sounded, A sig - nal boom from the gun;
The work is squarely be - fore us, The great decree handed down;
Take aim awhile, be stead - y, Be sure your aiming is low;

The staff and banner surround - ed, And vict - 'ry sure to be won.
We'll fire a thundering cho - rus In ev - 'ry cit - y and town.
And shoot whenever you're read- y, And then the sa- loon will go.

CHORUS.

Fire away, fire away with your ballots, Fire away, fire away on the field;

Fire away, fire away, fire away, fire away, Fire away, fire away till they yield.

Gentle Shepherd, Save Me Now.

HENRIETTA E. BLAIR.   WM. J. KIRKPATRICK.

1. Far a-way my steps have wandered, On the rugged mountain's brow;
2. Thou hast borne my weight of sorrow, At thy feet I humbly bow;
3. Though thy love I long have slighted, Though ungrateful I have been,
4. Though thy love I long have slighted, O'er my wasted years I weep;

But to thee my heart is cry-ing, Gen - tle Shepherd, save me now!
And my heart with thee is pleading, Gen - tle Shepherd, save me now!
To thy fold my faith has brought me; Let my weary   soul come in.
In thy blessed arms of mer - cy Shield and save thy wand'ring sheep.

D.S.—Un - to thee my heart is cry-ing, Gen - tle Shepherd, save me now!

CHORUS.   D.S.

Save me now! save me now! Gen - tle Shepherd, save me now!

Songs in the calm, still Night.

Jennie Garnett.

Jno. R. Sweney.

1. 'Tis the Lord who leadeth me still, 'Tis he who controls and governs my will,
2. 'Tis the Lord who whispers to me, I offered myself a ransom for thee;
3. Safe in him, I will not repine, Tho' trials and cares may sometimes be mine;
4. Safe in him, my hope and my all, Who tenderly hears whenever I call;

Crowns my life with holy delight, And giveth me songs in the calm, still night.
Say, what mean thy doubtings and fears; I carry thy sorrows and count thy tears.
He, I know, will guide me aright, Who giveth me songs in the calm, still night.
Safe in him, my burden is light, He giveth me songs in the calm, still night.

CHORUS.

O my soul, how favored thou art, Thus to come so near to his heart;

There by faith I walk in his light, Who giveth me songs in the calm, still night.

In the Hush of Early Morning. 89

Mrs. R. N. Turner.　　　　　　　　　　Wm. J. Kirkpatrick.

1. In the hush of ear-ly morning, When the breeze is whisp'ring low,
2. When the noontide falls up-on me, With its fer-vid light'ning ray,
3. As the dewy shades steal downward O'er the earth at evening mild,

There's a voice that gent-ly calls me, And its ac-cents well I know!
There's a voice, di-vine-ly earn-est, Bids me work while it is day;
There's a voice I love that whispers, "Af-ter la-bor, rest, my child!"

Here I am, O Saviour, wait-ing; For thy will a-lone is mine,
O-pen, Saviour, now be-fore me All thy will for me to do,
O my Saviour, lov-ing, ten-der, Help me to ac-count it blest

This is all my crown and glo-ry, I am thine, and on-ly thine!
On-ly help me, watching, working, Still to keep my Lord in view!
Thus to work within thy vineyard, Till thou call-est me to rest!

Ship of Zion.

Mrs. M. B. C. Slade.   Rev. D. Sullins, D D.

1. There's a wail from the islands of the sea, of the sea, There's a
2. There's a moan from the desert, full of pain, full of pain, There's a
3. There's a groan from the Ganges where they fall, where they fall, At the

voice that is calling you and me, you and me, In the old Ship of Zi-on,
sigh o-ver Afric's sunny plain, sun-ny plain, In the old Ship of Zi-on,
feet of the idols, in their thrall, in their thrall, In the old Ship of Zi-on,

The strong help of Zion, The good news of Zion, carry ye!
The strong help of Zion, Bear good news of Zion o'er the main.
The strong help of Zion, The good news of Zion, bear them all!

"Come o-ver and help us!" is the cry; is the cry; Come o-ver and
"Come o-ver and help us!" is the cry; is the cry; Come o-ver and
"Come o-ver and help us!" is the cry; is the cry; Come o-ver and

help us, or we die, or we die. I see the woe falling, I
help us, or we die, or we die. A-cross the wide waters, Hear
help us, or we die, or we die. I see i-dols falling, And

hear the voice calling, Oh, Ship of Sal - vation, thither fly.
Af- ric's dark daughters! Oh, Ship of Sal - vation, thither fly.
In - di - a calling, Oh, Ship of Sal - vation, thither fly.

Cling to the Mighty One.

L. L. PICKETT.

1. Cling to the Mighty One, Cling in thy grief; Cling to the
2. Cling to the Liv - ing One, Cling in thy woe; Cling to the
3. Cling to the Bleeding One, Cling to his side; Cling to the

Ho - ly One, He gives re - lief; Cling to the Gracious One,
Lov - ing One, Through all be - low; Cling to the Pard'ning One,
Ris - en One, In Him a - bide; Cling to the Com - ing One,

Cling in thy pain; Cling to the Faithful One, He will sustain.
He speaketh peace; Cling to the Healing One, Anguish shall cease.
Hope shall a - rise; Cling to the Reigning One, Joy lights thine eyes.

The Clear Light of Heaven.

F. A. B.

F. A. BLACKMER.

1. In darkness I wandered till Jesus I found, And then, praise his name! And
2. The birds o'er my head seemed to sing a new song, So wondrously sweet, So
3. And now we are walk-ing to-geth-er a-long, My Sa-viour and I, My
4. Oh, wonder-ful Brother, Redeemer and Friend! I love him I know, I

then, praise his name! The clear light of heaven my pathway shone round, And
wondrously sweet; All nature seemed praising in notes loud and long, My
Sa-viour and I; He blesses and leads me with hand kind and strong, And
love him I know; This blessed com-pan-ion-ship, nev-er to end, Grows

CHORUS.

peace to my spir-it there came.   And now I'm con-fid-ing, And
Saviour, when first we did meet.
free-ly his grace does sup-ply.
sweet-er as on-ward I go.

sweet-ly a-bid-ing   In Je-sus, my Sa-viour, Compan-ion and

Guide: His name I'm confess-ing,   He fills me with bless-ing; To me he's far dear - er Than all else be - side.

Sing Hallelujah.

G. E Lovelight.

Wm. J. Kirkpatrick.

1. When Je - sus washed my sins a - way, Sing hal - le - lu - jah!
2. He makes my wounded spir - it whole, Sing hal - le - lu - jah!

My hap - py heart be - gan to say, Praise ye the Lord.
He sat - is - fies my long - ing soul, Praise ye the Lord.

CHORUS.

Sing hal - lelu - jah! sing hallelujah! Sing hal - lelujah! praise ye the Lord.

3 I find him present everywhere,
  Sing hallelujah!
I cast on him my every care,
  Praise ye the Lord.

4 He keeps me safely by his side,
  Sing hallelujah!
I take him as my guard and guide,
  Praise ye the Lord.

5 No other good do I possess,
  Sing hallelujah!
He is my constant happiness,
  Praise ye the Lord.

6 And thus I journey day by day,
  Sing hallelujah!
Rejoicing on my heavenward way,
  Praise ye the Lord.

One by One.

Adapted from Mrs. Lydia Baxter.　　　　　　　　　　　　T. E. Perkins.

1. One by one we cross the riv - er, One by one we're passing o'er;
2. One by one we come to Je - sus, As we heed his gentle voice;
3. One by one the heavy - la - den Sink be - neath the noontide sun,

One by one the crowns are given On the bright and happy shore.
One by one his vineyard en - ter, There to la - bor and re - joice.
And the a - ged pilgrim welcomes Eve - ning shadows as they come;

Youth and childhood oft are pass - ing O'er the dark and rolling tide,
One by one sweet flowers we gather In the glorious work of love,—
One by one, with sins forgiv - en, May we stand upon the shore.

And the blessed Ho - ly Spir - it Is the dy - ing Christian's guide;
Garlands for the bless - ed Sav - iour Gather for the realms a - bove;
Waiting till the bless - ed Spir - it Takes our hand and guides us o'er;

And the loving, gen - tle Spir - it Bears them o'er the rolling tide.
And the loving, gen - tle Spir - it Bears them to our home of love.
And the loving, gen - tle Spir - it Leads us to the shining shore.

The Scarlet Line.

Rev. John O. Foster, B. D.

Jno. R. Sweney.

1. The blood of the Saviour for sin-ners was shed, In love and com-
2. When Christ was up-lift-ed, and mortals were shown Jehovah's far-
3. No more will the al-tars of vic-tims a-rise, Or flames from the

pas-sion divine; And now through the mercy of him who has bled, We
reach-ing design, How Jus-tice and Mer-cy were called to his throne, And
offerings shine; For life from the Lord has come down from the skies, That

D. S.—Mer-cy and Pardon for-ev-er have stood In
Faith quickly shouted her triumph in God, That
bound by the cords that for-ev-er remain, We

Fine.

fol - low the scar - let line. Our lives are pro-tect-ed with
bound by the scar - let line,— Then hope came to earth with a
ran through the scar - let line. O ho-ly, com-pas-sion-ate

love by the scar - let line.
came through the scar - let line.
trust in the scar - let line.

D. S.

pass-o-ver blood, Our walls with his cov-e-nants shine; While
heart-cheering word, And sung of this life-giv-ing sign; And
Lamb that was slain, We live in this bless-ing of thine, And,

The Unclouded Day.

(May be used as a Solo.)

Words and Melody by Rev. J. K. Alwood.　　　　Harmony by J. F. Kinsey.

1. O they tell me of a home far beyond the skies, O they tell me of a
2. O they tell me of a home where my friends have gone, O they tell me of that
3. O they tell me of the King in his beauty there, And they tell that mine
4. O they tell me that he smiles on his children there, And his smile drives their sor-

home far a-way; O they tell me of a home where no storm-clouds rise,
land far a-way; Where the tree of life in e-ter-nal bloom
eyes shall behold; Where he sits on the throne that is whiter than snow,
rows all a-way; And they tell me that no tears ever come a-gain,

O they tell me of an unclouded day; O the land of cloudless day,
Sheds its fragrance thro' the unclouded day; O the land of cloudless day,
In the cit-y that is made of gold; O that land mine eyes shall see,
In that lovely land of unclouded day; O that land of love-ly smiles,

O the land of an un-clouded sky; O they tell me of a
O the land of an un-clouded sky; O they tell me of my
O that land of an un-clouded sky; O they tell me of the
O the smiles of his love-beaming eye; O the King in his

home where no storm-clouds rise, O they tell me of an un - clouded day.
friends by the tree of life, In the land of the un - clouded day.
King on his snow-white throne, In the land of the un - clouded day.
beau- ty invites me there, To the land of the un - clouded day.

Whosoever.

JAMES NICHOLSON.   JNO. R. SWENEY.

1. I praise the Lord that one like me For mercy may to Je- sus flee,
2. I was to sin a wretched slave, But Jesus died my soul to save;
3. I look by faith and see this word, Stamp'd with the blood of Christ my Lord,
4. I now believe he saves my soul, His precious blood hath made me whole;

He says that who - so - ev - er will May seek and find sal- vation still.
He says that who - so - ev - er will May seek and find sal- vation still.
He says that who - so - ev - er will May seek and find sal- vation still.
He says that who - so - ev - er will May seek and find sal- vation still.

CHORUS.

My Saviour's promise faileth never; He counts me in the Whosoev- er.

From "Gems of Praise," by per.

98 I will Shout His Praise in Glory.

P. H. Dingman.

Jno. R. Sweney.

1. You ask what makes me happy, my heart so free from care, It is because my
2. I was a friendless wand'rer till Jesus took me in, My life was full of
3. I wish that ev'ry sinner before his throne would bow; He waits to bid them
4. I mean to live for Jesus while here on earth I stay, And when his voice shall

Sav - iour in mercy heard my prayer; He brought me out of darkness and
sor - row, my heart was full of sin; But when the blood so precious spoke
welcome, he longs to bless them now; If they but knew the rapture that
call me to realms of endless day, As one by one we gath - er, re-

now the light I see; O blessed, loving Saviour! to him the praise shall be.
pardon to my soul; Oh, blissful, blissful moment! 'twas joy beyond control.
in his love I see, They'd come and shout salvation, and sing his praise with me.
joicing on the shore, We'll shout his praise in glory, and sing forev - ermore.

CHORUS.

I will shout his praise in glo - ry, ... So will I, so will I, And we'll

all sing halle - lu-jah in heav-en by and by; I will shout his praise in

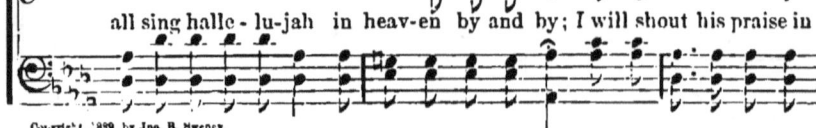

glo-ry, . . . And we'll all sing hallelujah in heaven by and by.

So will I, so will I,

Have You Something Good to Tell.

PRISCILLA J. OWENS.   WM. J. KIRKPATRICK.

Not too slow.

1. Have you something good to tell us, My Christian friend, to-day?
2. Have you something good to tell us Of Je-sus kind and true?
3. We are waiting now to hear you Proclaim his grace so free;

Tell how the Lord has met you, And helped you on your way.
Of hopes that reach to heav-en? Of mer-cies ev-er new?
Speak out and tell each sin-ner "His love has pardoned me."

CHORUS.

Tell of the lov-ing Sav-iour Who keeps us day by day;

Oh, tell of the pre-cious Saviour,—'Twill help us on our way.

The Whole Wide World.

Rev. J. Demster Hammond   Wm. J Kirkpatrick.

1. The whole wide world for Jesus, This shall our watchword be, Upon the highest
2. The whole wide world for Jesus, Inspires us with the thought That ev'ry son of
3. The whole wide world for Jesus, The marching order sound, Go ye and preach the
4. The whole wide world for Jesus, In the Father's home above Are many wondrous

mountain, Down by the widest sea. The whole wide world for Je-sus, To
Adam Hath by the blood been bought. The whole wide world for Jesus, O
gos-pel Wherev-er man is found. The whole wide world for Je-sus, Our
mansions, Mansions of light and love. The whole wide world for Je-sus, Ride

him all men shall bow, In ci-ty or on prairie, The world for Jesus now.
faint not by the way! The cross shall surely conquer In this our glorious day.
banner is unfurled, We bat-tle now for Jesus, And faith demands the world.
forth, O conquering king, Thro' all the mighty nations, The world to glory bring.

CHORUS.

The whole wide world, the whole wide world, Proclaim the gos-pel

tid-ings thro' the whole wide world, Lift up the cross for Je - sus, His

The Whole Wide World.—CONCLUDED 101

banner be unfurled, Till ev'ry tongue confess him, thro' the whole wide world.

Eternity!—Where?

A young man was working alone in a large room in which was a big clock, the loud ticking of which seemed to frame itself into the words, "Eternity!—where?" Unable to endure any longer the reflections thus awakened, he arose and stopped the clock; but the question, "Eternity!—where?" still so haunted him, that he threw down his work, and hurrying home, determined that he would not allow anything to engage his thoughts till he could satisfactorily answer that searching question, "Eternity!—where?"

JNO. R. SWENEY.

1. "E - ter - nity!—where?" It floats in the air; Amid clam-or or
2. "E - ter - nity!—where?" Oh! Eternity!—where? With redeemed ones in
3. "E - ter - nity!—where?" Oh! how can you share The world's giddy
4. "E - ter - nity!—where?" Oh! friend, have a care; Soon God will no
5. "E - ter - nity!—where?" Oh! Eter - nity!—where? Friend, sleep not, nor

si - lence it ev - er is there! The ques-tion so solemn—"E-
glo - ry? or fiends in de - spair? With one or the oth - er—"E-
pleasures, or heed-less-ly dare Do aught till you set - tle—"E-
long - er his judgment for - bear; This day may de - cide your "E-
take in the world an - y share, Till-you answer this question—"E-

rit. e dim.

ter - nity!—where?" The question so solemn—"E - ter - nity!—where?"
ter - nity!—where?" With one or the oth - er—"E - ter - nity!—where?"
ter - nity!—where?" Do aught till you settle—"E - ter - nity!—where?"
ter - nity!—where?" This day may decide your "E - ter - nity!—where?"
ter - nity!—where?" Till-you answer this question—"Eternity!—where?"

Copyright, 1888, by JOHN J. HOOD.

Sing, O Sing the Love of Jesus.

MAY CLIFTON. W. J. KIRKPATRICK.

1. Sing, O sing the love of Je - sus, Boundless, deep, unmeasured love;
2. Sing, O sing the love of Je - sus, Render hearty thanks and praise;
3. An - gel lips will join our an - them, Thro' the sky the sound prolong;
4. Pow'r and might and bliss e-ter - nal Now and ev - er-more shall be

Let the soul - in - spir-ing cho - rus Ring thro' all the courts a-bove.
While he gives us life and be - ing, Praise him on through endless days.
Heav'nly hosts take up the cho - rus, And with rap - ture swell the song.
Un - to him who loved and saved us With a love so full and free.

CHORUS.

Sing, O sing . . . . . the love of Je - - - - sus,
the love of Je - sus, Sing, O sing the love of Je - sus,

Heav'n and earth . . . . . . re - peat the strain;
re - peat the strain, Heav'n and earth re - peat the strain;

Sing, O sing, ... till ev - 'ry na - - - - tion
till ev - 'ry na - tion, Sing, O sing, till ev - 'ry na - tion

Ech - oes on . . . . the sweet re - frain.

the sweet re - frain,   Ech - oes on the sweet re- frain

The Beautiful Land.

H. E. ENGLE.

1. There's a beautiful land far beyond the sky, And Jesus my Saviour is there;
2. I have friends who have gone to that land on high,
They are free from all sorrow and care;
3. We shall meet in that beautiful land on high, And be with the bright and the fair;

He has gone to prepare me a home on high—Oh, I long, oh, I long to be there!
And I trust I shall meet them above the sky—Oh, I long, oh, I long to be there!
Where the waters of life sweetly murmur by—Oh, I long, oh, I long to be there!

CHORUS.

In that beau - - - - ti - ful land,   Where the an - gels stand,

In that beau - ti - ful land, In that beau - ti - ful land,

We shall meet,   We shall meet,   We shall meet in that beautiful land.

We shall meet   We shall meet,

Abiding and Confiding.

Rev. A. B. Simpson.   L. L. Pickett, alt.

1. I have learned the wondrous secret Of a-bid-ing in the Lord;
2. I am cru-ci-fied with Jesus, And he lives and dwells in me,
3. All my sick-ness-es I bring him, And he bears them all a-way;
4. For my words I take his wisdom, For my works his Spirit's power,

I have found the strength and sweetness, Of con-fid-ing in his word;
I have ceased from all my struggling, 'Tis no long-er I, but he;
All my fears and griefs I tell him, All my cares from day to day.
For my ways his gracious Presence Guards and guides me every hour.

I have tast-ed life's pure fountain, I am drinking of his blood,
All my will is yield-ed to him, And his Spir-it reigns within,
All my strength I draw from Je-sus, By his breath I live and move;
Of my heart he is the Portion, Of my joy the ceaseless Spring;

I have lost my-self in Je-sus, I am sinking in-to God.
And his precious blood each moment Keeps me cleansed and free from sin.
E'en his ver-y mind he gives me, And his faith, and life, and love.
Saviour, Sanc-ti-fi-er, Healer, Glorious Lord and com-ing King!

CHORUS.

I'm a-bid - - - - ing in the Lord,   And con-
I'm a-bid-ing in the Lord, I'm a-bid-ing in the Lord, And con-

fid - - - - ing in his word, And I'm hid - - -
fid - ing in his word, And con- fid - ing in his word And I'm hid- ing, safe- ly

- - - - ing, safe- ly hid - - - - ing, In the bos- om of his love.
hid - ing, I am hid - ing, safe- ly hid - ing,

Another Year.

FRANCES RIDLEY HAVERGAL.

L. L. PICKETT, alt.

1. An- oth- er year is dawning, Dear Master ; let it be In working or in
2. An- oth- er year of mercies, Of faithfulness and grace ; Another year of
3. An- oth- er year of service, Of witness of thy love ; Anoth- er year of

waiting, An- oth- er year with thee. An- oth- er year of lean- ing Up -
gladness In the shining of thy face. An- oth- er year of progress, An -
training For ho- lier work a - bove. An- oth- er year is dawning, Dear

on thy loving breast, Of ever- deep'ning trustfulness, Of quiet, hap- py rest.
other year of praise, Anoth- er year of prov- ing Thy presence "all the days."
Master, let it be   On earth, or else in heav - en, An- oth- er year for thee.

106 There's a Blessing for Me.

Henrietta E. Blair.   Wm. J. Kirkpatrick.

1. There is per - fect cleansing in the precious blood That flows for
2. I am saved each moment thro' the cleansing blood That now by
3. O the blood that keeps me from the power of sin My con-stant
4. There is life e - ter-nal in the precious blood That still is

all so free, There is full sal - va-tion in its crimson flood; There's a
faith I see; I am sweetly resting at the cross I love; There's a
theme shall be; I have laid my burden at the Saviour's feet; There's a
flow-ing free, And my soul shall glory in the Saviour's cross; There's a

CHORUS.

blessing from the Lord for me. There's a blessing for me, There's a

blessing for me, A blessing from the Lord for me; There is
for me,

full salvation in the crimson flood; There's a blessing from the Lord for me.

The Beautiful Light.

R. KELSO CARTER.   JNO R. SWENEY.

1. Je-sus is the light, the way, We are walking in the light, We are
2. We who know our sins forgiven, We are walking in the light, We are
3. As we journey here be - low, We are walking in the light, We are
4. We will sing his power to save, We are walking in the light, We are

walking in the light; Shining brighter day by day, We are walking in the
walking in the light; Find on earth the joy of heaven, We are walking in the
walking in the light; Oh, what joy and peace we know, We are walking in the
walking in the light; We will triumph o'er the grave, We are walking in the

REFRAIN.

beautiful light of God. We are walk - - ing in the light,   We are
                       Walking in the light,   beautiful light of God.

walk - - ing in the light,   We are walk - - ing in the
Walking in the light,   beau-ti-ful light of God,   Walking in the light,

light, ... We are walking in the beauti-ful light of God.
Walk-ing in the light,

The Precious Love of Jesus.

FANNY J. CROSBY.　　　　　　　　　　　　　WM. J. KIRKPATRICK.

1. O sing the power of love divine, The pre-cious love of Je-sus,
2. 'Tis love that conquers ev-'ry fear, The pre-cious love of Je-sus,
3. 'Tis love that fills the joyful heart, And draws it up to Je-sus,
4. When faith and hope have ceased to shine, And we are safe with Je-sus,

That bids the light in darkness shine, And wins the lost to Je-sus.
And now by faith has brought us near The bleed-ing side of Je-sus.
Where neith-er life nor death can part The sacred bonds from Je-sus.
We'll praise the power of love divine That brought us home to Je-sus.

CHORUS.

O precious, pure, unchanging love, The boundless love of Je-sus,

It binds our hearts in union sweet, And makes us one in Je sus.

More about Jesus.

E. E. HEWITT.　　　　　　　　　　　　　　　　JNO. R. SWENEY

1. More about Je-sus would I know, More of his grace to oth-ers show;
2. More about Je-sus let me learn, More of his ho - ly will discern,
3. More about Je-sus; in his word, Holding communion with my Lord:
4. More about Je-sus; on his throne, Riches in glo - ry all his own;

More of his sav-ing ful-ness see, More of his love who died for me.
Spir - it of God, my teacher　be, Showing the things of Christ to me.
Hearing his voice in　ev - 'ry line, Making each faithful say-ing mine.
More of his kingdom's sure increase; More of his coming, Prince of Peace.

REFRAIN.

More, more a-bout Je - sus, More, more a-bout Je - sus;

More of his sav-ing ful-ness see, More of his love who died for me.

110 Wondrous Glory.

Sallie M. Smith.   Jno. R. Sweney.

1. On the mount of wondrous glo - ry, Borne a - loft by faith, we stand,
2. On the mount of wondrous glo - ry, Where so oft 'tis ours to be.
3. On the mount of wondrous glo - ry, Where he bids us come and rest,
4. If on earth our souls are honored With such visions of delight,

While we drink the crystal wa - ters Flowing down from Eden's land.
In the brightness of his presence, Christ our Lord revealed we see.
Je - sus spreads a feast be - fore us, Making each a welcome guest.
Who can tell our heights of rap - ture, When our faith is lost in sight.

CHORUS.

How the heart its toil for- gets,
How the heart, its toil forgets,
In the

joy we there behold;
In the joy we there behold, there behold,
In the ful -

- - ness of his love,
ful - ness of his love, of his love,
That is bet - ter felt than told.

Mrs. M. A. W. Cooke.   L. L. Pickett.

1. In some way or other The Lord will provide; It may not be
2. At some time or other The Lord will provide; It may not be
3. Despond then no longer, The Lord will provide; And this be the
4. March on, then, right boldly, The sea shall divide; The pathway made

my way, It may not be thy way, And yet in his own way, "The
my time, It may not be thy time, And yet in his own time, "The
token— No word he hath spoken Was ev - er yet broken,—"The
glorious, With shoutings victorious, We'll join in the chorus, "The

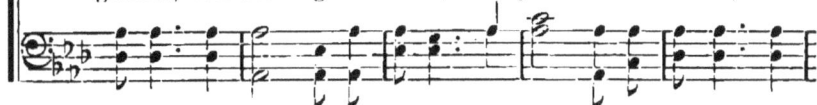

CHORUS.

Lord will provide." Then we'll trust in the Lord, And he will pro-

vide; Then we'll trust in the Lord, And he will provide.

Words of Jesus.

E. E. Hewitt. Wm. J. Kirkpatrick.

Matt. xi. 28. 1. Come unto me, the Saviour said, Come unto me, the Saviour said;
John xiv 6. 2. I am the way, the truth, the life, I am the way, the truth, the life;
Mark x. 21. 3. Take up the cross, and follow me, Take up the cross, and follow me;
Matt. vii. 7 4. Ask and it shall be given you, Ask and it shall be given you;

Come unto me, the Saviour said, And I will give you rest.
I am the way, the truth, the life, I am the light of the world. John viii. 12.
Take up the cross, and fol-low me, And thou shalt have treasure in heaven.
Ask and it shall be giv-en you, Seek and ye shall find.

CHORUS.

Oh, the blessed words of Je-sus! Precious words! hallowed words!

Oh, the blessed words of Je-sus! Words of life to me.

John iii. 36.
5 He that believeth | on the Son, :‖
Hath everlasting | life.

Is. xlv. 22.
6 Look unto me, and | be ye saved, :‖
All the ends of the | earth.

Matt. v. 8.
7 Blessed are the | pure in heart, :‖
For | they shall see | God.

Matt v. 12.
8 Re- | joice and be ex- | ceeding glad, :‖
For | great is your reward in | heaven.

John xiv. 18.
9 I | will not leave you | comfortless, ‖
I will come unto | you.
John vii. 37.
10 If | any man thirst let him | come unto
And drink of the water of | life. [me,:‖
Mark. x. 14.
11 Suffer little children to | come unto
me, :‖ [heaven.
For of | such is the kingdom of |
John xiv. 2.
12 I | go to prepare a | place for you, ‖
In my Fathers' house.

No Night Over There.

L. L. PICKETT.

Slowly and expressive.

1. No night shall be in heaven; no gath'ring gloom Shall o'er that glorious
2. No night shall be in heaven; for - bid to sleep, These eyes no more their
3. No night shall be in heaven, but endless noon; No fast de- clining
4. No night shall be in heaven; no darkened room, No bed of death, nor

landscape ev - er come; No tears shall fall in sadness o'er those flow'rs That
mournful vigils keep; Their fountains dried, their tears all washed away, They
sun, no waning moon; But there the Lamb shall yield perpetual light, 'Mid
silence of the tomb, But breezes ever fresh with love and truth Shall

CHORUS.

breathe their fragrance thro' celes - tial bowers. No night o - ver
gaze un - dazzled on e - ter - nal day.
pastures green and waters ev - er bright.
brace the frame with an immor - tal youth.

No night

there, In the cloudless realm of day, No night
o - ver there,

No night

o - ver there, Thro' the a - ges of e - ter - ni - ty.
o - ver there,

Cheerful Songs—H

A Perfect Salvation.

ANNA C. STOREY.   WM. J. KIRKPATRICK.

1. With a perfect sal-vation, through Jesus our Lord, We are saved by his
2. O, this perfect sal-vation is boundless and free, 'Tis the pledge of God's
3. On the cold, barren mountains O, why will you roam From the warm, loving
4. O, this perfect sal-vation is waiting for you, With a garment of

grace, and our faith in his word; 'Tis a gift he has purchased—his
mer - cy to you and to me; Then awake out of bondage, come
smile of a dear Father's home. Are you will - ing to trust him? then
praise it will clothe you a - new; It will give you a comfort no

blood it has cost; 'Tis a light in the darkness for souls that are lost.
forth at its voice, O'er a sinner re - turning let an - gels rejoice.
why not believe That a perfect sal - vation you now may receive?
oth - er can bring, It will seal you the children and heirs of a King.

REFRAIN.

Hear the song of rapture swelling, while the ransomed ones are telling Of the

precious blood of Je - sus, that will cleanse from eve - ry sin; Hear them shout the wondrous sto - ry : there is room   enough in   glo - ry, There is

room   e - nough in   glo - ry   for the world   to en - ter in.

My Home is in Heaven.

L. L. P.   L. L. PICKETT.

1.   My home is in heaven, Blest city a - bove ; Summer land of delight,
2.   God reigns in that cit- y, All glorious and fair, And its people are pure,
3.   Th'redeemed of all   a- ges In heaven shall meet, And we all shall unite

Of peace and of love, Summer land of de - light,   Of peace and of love.
No   sin enters there, And its people are   pure,   No   sin enters there.
To bow at his feet, And we all shall u - nite   To   bow at his feet.

4 Who made an atonement,
   And died on the tree
‖: To purchase salvation
   For sinners like me. :‖

5 Ah ! then I shall praise him,
   My Saviour and God,
‖: Who bought my soul's pardon
   With his precious blood. :‖

Are You Washed in the Blood?

E. A. H.   Rev. E. A. Hoffman. By per.

1. Have you been to Jesus for the cleansing power? Are you washed in the
2. Are you walking dai-ly ,by the Saviour's side? Are you washed in the
3. When the Bridegroom cometh will your robes be white, Pure and white in the
4. Lay a-side the garments that are stained with sin, And be washed in the

blood of the Lamb? Are you ful-ly trusting in his grace this hour? Are you
blood of the Lamb? Do you rest each moment in the Cru-ci-fied? Are you
blood of the Lamb? Will your soul be ready for the mansions bright, And be
blood of the Lamb? There's a fountain flowing for the soul unclean, O be

CHORUS.

washed in the blood of the Lamb? Are you washed   in the

Are you washed

blood,   In the soul-cleansing blood of the Lamb?   Are your

in the blood,   *of the Lamb?*

garments spotless? are they white as snow? Are you washed in the blood of the Lamb?

# Come, ye Blessed.

FANNY J. CROSBY. WM. J. KIRKPATRICK.

1. When our Saviour in his glo-ry With the an-gel host shall come,
   When in clouds from heaven descending He shall call his children home,
2. To the well of liv-ing wa-ter If the thirsty we have led,
   If the stranger we have sheltered, And the hungry we have fed,
3. If we give our lives to Je-sus And delight to do his will,
   If we fol-low out his teaching, And his great commands ful-fil,

When be-fore him shall be gath-ered All the na-tions far and near,
If a wea-ry, faint-ing broth-er We have tried to help and cheer,
If our light is seen by oth-ers, Like the noonday bright and clear,

What a shout of joy will greet him, When the welcome words we hear:
Oh, the rest that we shall ent-er, When the welcome words we hear:
What a joy-ful, joy-ful meet-ing, When the welcome words we hear:

CHORUS. (Matt. xxv. 34.)

Come, ye bless-ed of my Fa-ther, Come, ye bless-ed of my Fa-ther, In-

her-it the kingdom prepared for you From the foundation of the world.

There's a Great Day Coming.

W. L. T.　　　　　　　　　　　　　　　　　　　W. L. Thompson.

1. There's a great day com-ing, A great day com-ing, There's a great day coming by and by, When the saints and the sinners shall be part-ed right and left, Are you read-y for that day to come?

2. There's a bright day com-ing, A bright day com-ing, There's a bright day coming by and by, But its brightness shall on-ly come to them that love the Lord, Are you read-y for that day to come?

3. There's a sad day com-ing, A sad day com-ing, There's a sad day coming by and by, When the sinner shall hear his doom, "De-part, I know ye not," Are you read-y for that day to come?

CHORUS.

Are you read-y? are you read-y? Are you read-y for the judgment day? Are you ready? are you ready For the judgment day?

By permission of W. L. Thompson & Co., East Liverpool, O.

Meet in the Morning.

H. F. BLAIR. WM. J. KIRKPATRICK.

1. We are marching onward to the heavenly land, To meet each other in the morning;
2. We are trav'ling onward from a world of care, To meet each other in the morning;
3. We are trav'ling onward, and the way grows bright, We'll meet each other in, etc.,

We are pressing forward to the golden strand, Where joy will crown us in the morning.
Oh, the time is coming, we shall soon be there, And joy will crown us in the morning.
Where our friends are waiting, at the gate of life, And joy will crown us in the, etc.,

CHORUS.

In the morning, in the morning, We will gather with the faithful in the morning;

Where the night of sorrow shall be rolled away, And joy will crown us in the morning.

4 Where the hills are blooming on the other shore,
We'll meet each other in the morning!
Where the heart's deep longing will be felt no more,
And joy will crown us in the morning.

5 In the boundless rapture of a Saviour's love
We'll meet each other in the morning;
Then we'll sing his glory in the realms above,
And joy will crown us in the morning.

The City of Light.

A. S. K.

A. S. KIEFFER. By per.

1. There's a cit - y of light 'mid the stars, we are told, Where they know not a
   And the gates are of pearl, and the streets are of gold, And the building ex-

2. Brother dear, nev- er fear,—we shall triumph at last, If we trust in the
   When our tri - als and toils, and our weepings are past, We shall meet in that

sor- row or care:
ceed- ing- ly fair.
word he has giv'n;
home up in heav'n.

CHORUS.

Let us pray for each oth- er, nor faint by the way,

In this sad world of sor - row and care, For that home is so

bright, and is al - most in sight, And I trust in my heart you'll go there.

3 Sister dear, never fear,—for the Saviour is near,
    With his hand he will lead you along;
  And the way that is dark Christ will graciously clear,
    And your mourning shall turn to a song.

4 Let us walk in the light of the gospel divine;
    Let us ever keep near to the cross;
  Let us love, watch, and pray, in our pilgrimage here;
    Let us count all things else but as loss.

It Just Suits Me.

E. E. Hewitt.   Wm. J. Kirkpatrick.

1. What a wonder - ful salvation! For its length and breadth and height
2. Oh, this blessed "who-so - ev - er," Calling ev - 'ry one who will,
3. Precious promis - es of Je - sus, Sweeping ev - 'ry human need!
4. What a perfect, present Saviour! What a true and loving friend!

Far ex - cel the grandest knowledge Of the ser - a- phim in light;
To the sparkling, liv - ing waters, Flowing ful - ly, free - ly still;
For the grace of our Redeem- er Must our high - est thought exceed;
Can we ev - er praise him rightly? Tell how grace and glo - ry blend?

I can nev - er, nev - er fathom Half its ho - ly mys - ter - y,
No, I know not why he loves me, But his blood is all my plea;
To the mighty, roy - al storehouse Let me use the gold - en key,
Now the Prince of Peace is reigning, O - ver - rul-ing all I see;

CHORUS.

But I know it is for sinners, And it just suits me. It just suits
I can trust his "whoso- ev - er," For it just suits me.
Find the special, tender promise That will just suit me.
So, whatev - er lot he orders, May it just suit me.

me, It just suits me, This wonderful salvation, It just suits me.

In the Secret of His Presence.

Rev. Henry Burton, M. A.

Jno. R. Sweney.

Moderato.

1. In the se-cret of his presence I am kept from strife of tongues;
2. In the se-cret of his presence All the darkness dis-ap-pears;
3. In the se-cret of his presence Nev-er-more can foes a-larm;
4. In the se-cret of his presence Is a sweet, un-bro-ken rest;

His pa-vil-ion is around me, And with-in are cease-less songs!
For a sun, that knows no setting, Throws a rainbow on my tears.
In the sha-dow of the Highest I can meet them with a psalm:
Pleasures, joys, in glorious ful-ness, Making earth like Ed-en blest:

Storm-y winds his word ful-fil-ing, Beat without, but can-not harm,
So the day grows ev-er light-er, Broad'ning to the per-fect noon;
For the strong pa-vil-ion hides me, Turns their fier-y darts a-side,
So my peace grows deep and deeper, Widening as it nears the sea,

For the Master's voice is stilling Storm and tem-pest to a calm.
So the day grows ev-er brighter, Heav'n is com-ing, near and soon.
And I know, whate'er be-tides me, I shall live be-cause he died!
For my Sav-iour is my Keep-er, Keeping mine and keep-ing me!

Copyright, 1885, by Jno. R. Sweney.

FANNY J. CROSBY. WM. J. KIRKPATRICK.

1. There is healing at the fount-ain, Come, behold the crimson tide,
2. There is healing at the fount-ain, Come and find it, wea-ry soul,
3. There is healing at the fount-ain, Look to Je-sus now and live,
4. There is healing at the fount-ain, Precious fountain filled with blood,

Flowing down from Calvary's mountain, Where the Prince of Glory died.
There your sins may all be cov - ered; Je - sus waits to make you whole.
At the cross lay down your bur- den; All your wanderings he'll forgive,
Come, O come, the Saviour calls you; Come and plunge beneath its flood.

CHORUS.

O the fountain! blessed, healing fountain! I am glad 'tis flowing free,

O the fountain! precious, cleansing fountain! Praise the Lord, it cleanseth me.

The Lord is Rich in Mercy.

E. A. BARNES. "Great are thy tender mercies, O Lord."—Ps. cxix. 156. Jno. R. SWENEY.

1. Oh, the Lord is rich in mer - cy, As his word will sweetly show,
2. Oh, the Lord is rich in mer - cy, As he reigns in life a - bove,
3. Oh, the Lord is rich in mer - cy, As we all may see and know,

And the fount will nev - er fail us In its free and bless - ed flow;
And we know 'tis sweetly blend - ed With his ho - ly name of love;
And he waits to hear us call - ing, Tender mer - cy to be - stow;

We have grieved the Holy Spir - it, Heeding not his lov - ing call,
As we all are weak and sin - ful, He will prove a friend in - deed,
We are prone to sin and er - ror, We are prone to go a - stray,

Yet, in bringing true con - tri - tion There is mer - cy for us all.
And his mer - cy, ev - er flow - ing, Meets our ev - 'ry want and need.
Yet his mer - cy it will reach us, And will bring us home to - day.

CHORUS.

Oh, there is mer - cy for all, yes, for all, Mer - cy for you, mercy for me; Oh, there is mer - cy for all, Mer - cy for you and me.

yes, for all,

Moments of Blessing.

FANNY J. CROSBY. JNO. R. SWENEY.

1. Rich are the moments of blessing Je-sus my Saviour be-stows;
2. Rich are the moments of blessing, Lovely, and hallowed, and sweet,
3. Why should I ev - er grow weary? Why should I faint by the way?
4. Though by the mist and the shadow Sometimes my sky may be dim,

Fine.

Pure is the well of sal - vation Fresh from his mercy that flows.
When from my la - bor at noontide Calm-ly I rest at his feet.
Has he not promised to give me Strength for the toils of the day?
Rich are the moments of blessing Spent in communion with him.

D.S.—Spreading a beau - ti - ful rainbow O - ver the val - ley of tears.

D.S.

CHORUS.

Ev - - er he walketh beside me, Bright - ly his sunshine appears,

Ev - er, yes, ev - er he walk-eth be-side me, Brightly his sunshine, his sunshine appears,

Waiting at the Pool.

Rev. A. J. Hough.   Wm. G. Fischer.   By per.

1. Thousands stand to-day in sorrow, Waiting at the pool; Saying they will
2. Souls your filthy garments wearing, Waiting at the pool; Hearts your heavy
3. Thousands once were standing near you, Waiting at the pool; Come their voices
4. Mother leaves the son, the daughter, Waiting at the pool; Calls to them a-
5. Step in boldly—death may smite you, Waiting at the pool: Jesus may no

wash to-morrow, Waiting at the pool; Oth- ers step in left and right,
bur- den bearing, Waiting at the pool; Can it be you nev- er heard,
back to cheer you, Waiting at the pool; Back from Canaan's happy shore,
cross the water, Waiting at the pool; You can nev - er more embrace
more invite you, Waiting at the pool; Faith is near you, take her hand,

Wash their stained garments white, Leav- ing you in sorrow's night,
Jesus long a - go hath stirred-The wa - ters with his might- y word,
Sor - rows past and la - bor o'er, Where they stand in tears no more,
Moth - er or be - hold her face, If you keep the lep - er's place.
Seek with her the bet - ter land, And no long - er doubting stand

Waiting at the pool, Waiting, wait- ing, waiting at the pool.

'Tis so Sweet to Trust in Jesus.

Mrs. Louisa M. R. Stead.   Wm. J. Kirkpatrick.

1. 'Tis so sweet to trust in Je-sus, Just to take him at his word;
2. O, how sweet to trust in Je-sus, Just to trust his cleansing blood;
3. Yes, 'tis sweet to trust in Je-sus, Just from sin and self to cease;
4. I'm so glad I learned to trust thee, Precious Je-sus, Saviour, Friend;

Just to rest up-on his promise; Just to know, "Thus saith the Lord."
Just in sim-ple faith to plunge me 'Neath the healing, cleansing flood.
Just from Je-sus simp-ly tak-ing Life and rest, and joy and peace.
And I know that thou art with me, Wilt be with me to the end.

REFRAIN.

Je-sus, Je-sus, how I trust him! How I've proved him o'er and o'er!

Je-sus, Je-sus, precious Je-sus! O for grace to trust him more.

From "Songs of Triumph," by per.

"Overcomers."

W. J. K.

WM. J. KIRKPATRICK.

QUESTION.

1 John v. 5. 1. Who, who is he? Who, who is he? Who, who is he that o‑ver‑

Rev. iii. 5. 2. What shall he wear? What shall he wear? What shall he wear that over‑

Rev. ii. 7. 3. What shall he eat? What shall he eat? What shall he eat that o‑ver‑

Rev. iii. 12. 4. What shall he be? What shall he be? What shall he be that o‑ver‑

com‑eth by the blood of the Lamb? He that be‑liev‑eth and is

com‑eth by the blood of the Lamb? He shall be clothed in

com‑eth by the blood of the Lamb? He shall eat of the

com‑eth by the blood of the Lamb? He shall be a pil‑lar in the

RESPONSE.

born of God, He that be‑liev‑eth and is born of God,

rai‑ment white, He shall be clothed in rai‑ment white,

tree of life, He shall eat of the tree of life,

tem‑ple of God, He shall be a pil‑lar in the temple of God,

He that believeth and is born of God, Shall overcome by the blood.

He shall be clothed in raiment white, That overcomes by the blood.

He shall eat of the tree of life, That overcomes by the blood.

He shall be a pillar in the temple of God, That overcomes by the blood.

O, the precious, precious blood! O, the cleansing, healing flood!

O, the pow'r and the love of God, Thro' the blood of the Lamb!

Rev. iii. 5.

5 ‖:What shall he hear?:‖ that over-
By the blood of the Lamb? [cometh
‖:He shall hear his name con-|fessed in
heaven, :‖
That overcomes by the blood.

Rev. xxi. 7.

6 ‖:What shall he have?:‖ that over-
By the blood of the Lamb? [cometh
‖:God will give him all things, and|
make him his son, :‖
That overcomes by the blood.

Rev. iii 21.

7 ‖:Where shall he sit?:‖ that over-
By the blood of the Lamb? [cometh
‖:He shall sit with | Jesus, on his
throne, :‖
That overcomes by the blood

1 John v. 4.

8 ‖:What is the victory?:‖ that over-
By the blood of the Lamb? [cometh
‖:Faith is the victory that | over-
cometh, ‖:
By the blood of the Lamb.

129 All the way long it is Jesus.

1. { O good old way, how sweet thou art! All the way long it is Je-sus;
May none of us from thee de-part; All the way long it is Je-sus. }

CHORUS.

Je-sus, Je-sus, Why, all the way long it is Je-sus.

2 But may our actions always say
We're marching in the good old way.

3 This note above the rest shall swell,
That Jesus doeth all things well.

At the Beautiful Gate.

Rev. J. H. Martin.   R. M. McIntosh. By per.

1. { I think I should mourn o'er my sor-row-ful fate, If sor-row in
   { If no one should be at the beau-ti-ful gate, There waiting and

CHORUS.

heav-en can be. } "Yes, wait - - ing and watching for
watching for me, } Yes, waiting and watching for me, for

me, Yes, wait - - ing and watching for me; May ma-ny of
me, Yes, waiting and watching for me, for me;

those at the beauti-ful gate Be wait-ing and watching for me.

2.
How sadly I'd feel in the heavenly state,
  If sadness in heaven can be.
If no one should be at the beautiful gate,
  Conducted to glory by me.

3.
O Lord, I beseech thee for wisdom and
  In winning lost souls unto thee. [grace,
That many may be in that beautiful place,
  A crown of rejoicing to me.

He is My Portion Forever.

Lizzie Edwards

Jno. R. Sweney.

1. All, all to Je-sus, I consecrate a - new, He is my portion for-ev - er;
2. All, all to Je-sus, my trusting heart can say, He is my portion for ev - er;
3. Tho' he may try me this blessed truth I know, He is my portion for-ev - er;
4. All, all to Je-sus, I cheerfully re-sign, He is my portion for-ev - er;

On-ly his glory henceforth will I pursue, He is my portion for-ev - er.
Led by his mercy I'm walking ev'ry day, He is my portion for-ev - er.
He will not leave me, his promise tells me so, He is my portion for-ev - er.
I have the witness that he, my Lord, is mine, He is my portion for-ev - er.

REFRAIN.

Take, take the world with all its gilded toys, Take, take the world, I covet not its joys,

Mine is a wealth no moth nor rust destroys; Jesus my portion forev - er.

Marching On to Victory.

Nathan Dun, D. D. TEMPERANCE SONG. Wm. J. Kirkpatrick.

1. The temperance cause is moving on, Our State and nation shall be free;
2. Thy kingdom come, O Lord, we pray; 'Tis coming soon, the world shall see;
3. The temperance banner soon shall wave From north to south, from sea to sea:

A better day begins to dawn: We're marching on to victo - ry!
God save our homes, we cry to-day, While marching on to victo - ry.
With earnest step, ye true and brave, We're marching on to victo - ry!

CHORUS.

We're marching on, ... we're marching on, ... We're marching

on . . . to vic-to-ry; . . . . A better day . . . begins to
We're marching on to vic-to-ry, to vic-to-ry,

dawn, . . . We are marching, marching on to victory.
on . . . to vic-to-ry.
to vic-to-ry.

4 We soon shall join the glad refrain :
   "The land we love at last is free!
   Hosanna! swell the joyful strain!"
   We're marching on to victory!

5 The crowning work will soon be done :
   God speed the coming jubilee!
   Behold, the day is almost won!
   We're marching on to victory!

Home to Mother in Heaven.

A. S. K.

A. S. KIEFFER. By per.

1. O father, come kiss me once more, And watch by my bed just to night,
2. O father, what news shall I take   To Jesus and mother, for you?
3. Our home here is lonely and dark,   And oft we are hungry and cold;

Your Nettie will walk thro' the Valley of Death, Ere dawn of the sweet Sabbath light.
I'll tell him to send holy angels of light To bless and to comfort you too.
But I shall go home to my mother to-night, Where pleasures are purer than gold.

CHORUS.

O   father, I'm go-ing to   mother so dear,   I dreamed that I

saw her last   night; And   o-ver the riv-er sweet voices I hear, They

call me to mansions of light,—Home,   home, home to my mother in heaven.

4 O father, dear father, once more
  Of Jesus I pray you to think:
  And when I am gone to my mother in
    heaven,
  O father, please give up your drink.

5 O father, dear father, once more
  Please read in my Bible, and think:
  "No drunkard shall enter the kingdom
    of heaven,"
  O God, keep my father from drink !

Touch Not, nor Taste.

Mrs. M. B. C. Slade.   R. M. McIntosh. By per.

1. Say, who hath sor-row, con-tentions and woe? They where the wine-
2. Say, who in spir-it are wounded, in pain? They who go seek-
3. Say, who is stricken un-til he must be Like as one toss'd
4. What shall we tell them, oh, what can we say? How can we turn

cup   is   flow-ing who go: Look not up-on it, a
ing   the wine-cup a-gain; Tar-ry-ing long till the
in   the midst of the sea? They who are beat-en and
them from sin-ning a-way? Lov-ing-ly give them the

ser-pent its head Hides in the glow of the glit-ter-ing red.
spar-kle is past, Lo, it shall sting like an ad-der at last.
sick-ened and sore, They who have fall-en the wine-cup be-fore.
broth-er-ly hand, Ten-der-ly help-ing the fall-en to stand.

REFRAIN.

Touch not, nor taste, touch not, nor taste: Oh, from the ad-

der that sting-eth you, haste! Tar-ry nor stay,

tar - ry nor stay, There when a ser-pent but hides to be - tray.

The Wages of Sin.

W. J. K.

WM. J. KIRKPATRICK.

1. I have labored for thee, O sin, With en-er-gy, night and day,
2. But I've given my youth and strength, My talents and time to thee,
3. I have slighted the voice of God, And stilled my conscience too;
4. I have severed the ties of earth, And ruined my hopes of heaven,

Now what shall I have for my reward, And what is my utmost pay?
I have bartered away my words of truth, And nothing remains to me.
I have done despite to the Spirit's power, In striving thy work to do.
And only for thee I've lived and toiled, And now, what reward is given?

CHORUS.

"The wages of sin is death," All that is promised, you know,—

ad lib.   *rit.*

p   *pp*

Nothing but death, e - ter-nal death, Bit-ter remorse and woe.

136 Coming Home.

Rev. J. P. Dimmitt.   W. J. Kirkpatrick.

1. We have wandered far a - way from our Father's home, In the
2. We are coming now by faith, by the Spir - it led, We are
3. We have kindred gone be- fore, to the heavenly home, And they

dark and dreary paths of sin; But we hear our Saviour's voice calling
coming with our hearts to thee; We are trusting in the blood that for
draw us by the chords of love; They are calling us to - day, calling

REFRAIN.

us to come, And at once a better life be- gin. We are coming home,
us was shed, And the Holy Spirit sets us free.
us to come To the happy, happy home above.   coming,

We are coming home, coming home to - day; We have
coming,   coming.   to - day,

heard thy loving voice, Blessed Saviour, and rejoice; We are coming home to-day.

He's Mighty to Save.

E. E. Hewitt. Isaiah lxiii. 1. Wm. J. Kirkpatrick.

1. Je - sus is wait-ing his grace to be-stow; Sin "red like crimson" he
2. Standing a - lone in the strife we shall fail, Close to our Leader his
3. Take him the burden that weighs on your heart, Take him the trouble, he'll
4. Up from the val - ley the darkness is gone When Jesus brings there the

makes white as snow; Lov - ing us free - ly, his life - blood he gave;
might will pre - vail; Or if a bless-ing for oth - ers we crave,
com - fort im-part; Held by his hand we can walk on the wave;
beau - ty of dawn; Vic - t'ry, glad vic - t'ry, we sing o'er the grave!

CHORUS.

Bless - ed Redeem - er! he's might - y to save. Might - y to save,
Pray on, be - liev-ing,—he's might - y to save.
Look up to Je - sus, he's might - y to save.
Glo - ry to Je - sus! he's might - y to save.

might - y to save, Je - sus is might-y to save;

is might - y to save, he is

Might-y to save, mighty to save, Je - sus is mighty to save.

138 No Burdens Allowed to Pass Through.

A London gateway is inscribed, "No burdens allowed to pass through." The same words are inscribed in living light over the gate into the "Highway of Holiness."—Rev. E. I. D. Pepper.

ABBIE MILLS.   Isaiah xxxv. 1, 2.   Dr. H. L. Gilmour.

1. Where deserts abundant-ly bloom, And souls full of mu-sic are found,
2. This ho-ly and beauti-ful way No ravenous beast can pass o'er;
3. Redeemed ones with garments made clean, In blood that was shed for the lost,
4. Here songs interwov-en with joy On the heads of the ransomed a-bide,

Who journey along day by day, Tasting fruits that in Canaan a-bound,
The foot that's unclean is debarred From touching that crystal-paved floor;
Walk there with a comfort unknown Before they the threshhold had crossed;
While nearing the Zion a-bove, Just floating on love's silv'ry tide.

A way is cast up for our feet By Je-sus the faithful and true,
But wayfaring men shall not err Who keep on-ly Je-sus in view,
Cross o-ver! away with your fear! Oh, glory! there's room there for you;
Be care-ful for nothing, be-loved, For Je-sus still car-eth for you;

Fine

And over the gateway is always inscribed, "No burdens allowed to pass thro'."
And read what is written, so truthful and clear, "No burdens allowed to pass thro'."
And still at the gateway you ever will hear, "No burdens allowed to pass thro'."
See! there on the arch, wrote in letters of light, "No burdens allowed to pass thro'."

D. S.—Leave all at the cross, there by Calvary's tree, No burdens allowed to pass thro'

CHORUS. *D.S.*

No burdens allowed to pass through, No burdens, no burdens with you;

Vale of Beulah.

E. A. HOFFMAN. JOSEPH GARRISON

1. { I am passing down the val - ley that they say is so lone,
   { 'Tis to me the vale of Beu - lah, 'tis a beau - ti - ful way,
2. { Not a shad - ow, not a shad - ow ev - er dark - ens the way,
   { And the mu - sie, sweetly chanted by the heav - en - ly throng,
3. { So I journey with re - joic - ing toward the Cit - y of Light,
   { And I near the o - pen por - tals of the kingdom a - bove,

D.S. Fine.

But I find that all the pathway is with flow'rs o - ver-grown; }
For the Saviour walks be - side me, my compan - ion all day. }
For a radiance of rare glo - ry shines up - on it all day: }
Floats in ca - dence down the val - ley, and it cheers me a - long. }
While each day my joy is deep - er, and the path grows more bright; }
For this highway leads to Ca - naan, to the Kingdom of Love. }

D.S.—For the love - ly land of Ca - naan In the dis - tance I see.

CHORUS. *D.S*

Vale of Beulah! Vale of Beulah! Thou art precious to me;

Glory to God, Hallelujah!

Fanny J. Crosby.   Wm. J. Kirkpatrick.

1. We are nev-er, nev-er wea-ry of the grand old song; Glo-ry to
2. We are lost a-mid the rapture of redeem-ing love; Glo-ry to
3. We are go-ing to a palace that is built of gold; Glo-ry to
4. There we'll shout redeeming mercy in a glad, new song; Glo-ry to

God, hal-le-lu-jah! We can sing it loud as ever, with our faith more strong:
God, hal-le-lu-jah! We are rising on its pinions to the hills a-bove;
God, hal-le-lujah! Where the King in all his splendor we shall soon behold:
God, hallelujah! There we'll sing the praise of Jesus with the blood-wash'd throng:

Fine. CHORUS.

Glo-ry to God, hal-le-lu-jah! O, the children of the Lord have a

right to shout and sing, For the way is grow-ing bright, and our

D.S.

souls are on the wing; We are going by and by to the palace of a King!

Come and See.

Charles H. Elliott.　　　　　　　　　　　　　　Jno. R. Sweney.

1. There is pardon sweet, at the Master's feet, Come and see, O come and see;
2. There's an easy yoke that you all may bear, Come and see, O come and see;
3. There's a healing balm for the weary breast, Come and see, O come and see
4. There's a life beyond, 'tis a life di - vine, Come and see, O come and see

CHORUS.

There's a song of peace that shall never cease, Come, O come and see.　In the
There's a ho- ly joy that you all may share, Come, O come and see.
There's a tranquil peace and a sa-cred rest, Come, O come and see.
And the light of faith on your path will shine, Come, O come and see.

precious, precious blood of Je - sus Washed a - way　　your sins may be;

You may plunge just now in its cleansing flood,—Come, will you come and see.

I Have Come to the Fountain.

In that day there shall be a fountain opened for sin and for uncleanness.

Rev. WM. M. CARR.   W. J. KIRKPATRICK.

1. I was once far a - way from my Saviour, Far a - way from his
2. His Spir - it sought out my poor refuge, Sent con - vic - tion and
3. Just now I plunge in - to the fountain, Just now I hear,
4. I will bless him for - ev - er and ev - er Who saved a poor

kind, loving care; I had injured him times without number, I was
knowledge of sin, I sought for my Lord till I found him, And
"go, sin no more," My heart is washed clean, I will praise him! My
reb - el like me, In life will proclaim him to others, And

CHORUS.

down in the depths of despair.   I have come to the Fountain of
knew that my soul was redeemed.
soul as an ea - gle doth soar.
praise him e - ter - nal - ly.

cleansing, To the Fountain of cleansing from sin; Washed and made

free from all sin would I be, Just now I am en - tering in.

Glory to Jesus, He Saves.

P. B.

P. BILHORN.

1. Glo - ry to Je - sus who died on the tree, Paid the great price that my
2. Once in my heart there was sin and despair, Now the dear Saviour him-
3. Come, then, ye wea - ry, who long to be free, Come to the Saviour, he

soul might be free; Now I can sing hal - le - lu - jah to God,
self dwelleth there, And from his pres - ence comes peace to my soul,
wait - eth for thee; Then with the ransomed this song you can sing,

CHORUS.

Glo - ry! he saves, he saves. Glo - ry! he saves, glo - ry! he saves,

Saves a poor sin - ner like me; Glo - ry! he saves,

glo - ry! he saves, Saves a poor sin - ner like me, like me.

Ring Out the Hallelujahs.

Miss Emma M. Johnston. Wm. J. Kirkpatrick.

1. Sing the song the ransomed sing, Let your hal-le-lujahs ring,
2. Sing the love that set you free; Sing the song of lib-er-ty,
3. Sing the grace that made you whole; Sing the vict'ries of the soul,
4. Sing till heaven shall catch the strain, Hallelu-jah yet a-gain,

Glo-ry to the Lord your King; Ring out the halle-lujahs.
Sing the glo-ry yet to be; Ring out the hal-le-lujahs.
Sing while time shall onward roll; Ring out the hal-le-lujahs.
"Love redeeming" the refrain; Ring out the hal-le-lujahs.

REFRAIN.

Hal-le-lu-jah! . . . . Hal-le-lu-jah! . . . .
Hal-le-lu-jah!   Hal-le-lu-jah!

Glo-ry to our Lord and King; Ring out the halle-lu-jahs.

Jesus is Good to Me.

Rev. E. H. Stokes. D. D.   Jno. R. Sweney.

1. I love my Saviour, his heart is good, He has loved me o'er and o'er;
2. He calls, I rise, and he maketh me whole,—How fond his tender embrace!
3. I want to love him with all my heart, Tho' all its powers are small;
4. He's good to me in my sorrow's night, He's good in the tempest's roll;

He sought me wand'ring, I'm saved by his blood, And I love him more and more.
He cleanses and keeps me and blesses my soul'—My day the smile of his face.
I will not keep from him any part, For he is worthy of all.
He bringeth from darkness into light,—With joy he filleth my soul.

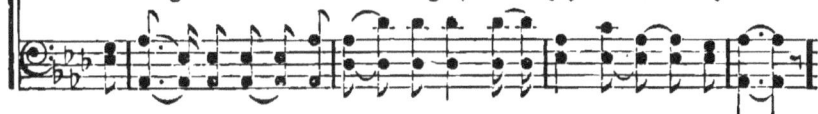

CHORUS.

Je - sus is good to me, . . . Je - sus is good to me; . . .
to me,   to me;

So good! so good! Je - sus is good to my soul.

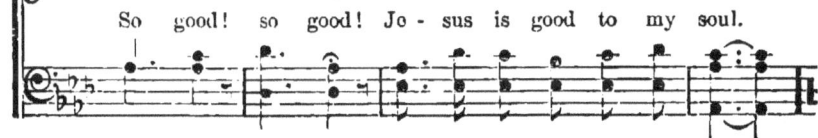

146 Only Believe.

EMMA M. JOHNSTON.   Mark v. 36.   WM. J. KIRKPATRICK.

1. Oh, why should we wres - tle with fears And doubts, which the
2. His word is as - sur - ance com - plete; Thy sins and thine
3. How ea - sy the terms of his grace: 'Tis on - ly to

Spir - it must grieve? And why should we languish in sor - row and tears,
i - dols now leave; Come, pleading his promise, and fall at his feet,
ask and re - ceive; The seal of his fav - or, the smile of his face,

When there's nothing to do but be - lieve.
Then you've nothing to do but be - lieve.
Are for those who will on - ly be - lieve.

CHORUS.

Be - lieve, be-
Be - lieve, be-lieve,

lieve, On - ly on Je - sus be - lieve; Sal - va - tion is

be - lieve,

wait - ing for you and for me. There is nothing to do but be - lieve.

Copyright, 1889, by Wm. J. Kirkpatrick.

Blessed Assurance.

F. J. Crosby. "He is faithful that hath promised."—Heb. x. 23. Mrs. Jos. F. Knapp.

1. Blessed as-surance, Jesus is mine! Oh, what a foretaste of
2. Perfect sub-mis-sion, perfect de - light, Visions of rap - ture
3. Perfect sub-mis-sion, all is at rest, I in my Saviour am

glory di - vine! Heir of sal - va - tion, purchase of God, Born of his
burst on my sight, Angels descend-ing, bring from a - bove Echoes of
happy and blest, Watching and waiting, looking a - bove, Filled with his

CHORUS.

Spir - it, washed in his blood. This is my sto - ry, this is my
mer - cy, whispers of love.
goodness, lost in his love.

song, Praising my Sav - iour all the day long; This is my

sto - ry, this is my song, Praising my Saviour all the day long.

My Jesus, I Love Thee.

"Mine are thine and thine are mine."
John xvii. 10.

"London Hymn Book."

A. J. GORDON. By per.

1. My Je - sus, I love thee, I know thou art mine,
2. I love thee be - cause thou have first lov - ed me,
3. I will love thee in life, I'll love thee in death,
4. In man - sions of glo - ry and end - less delight,

For thee all the fol - lies of sin I re - sign;
And pur - chased my par - don on Cal - va - ry's tree;
And praise thee as long as thou lend - est me breath;
I'll ev - er a - dore thee in heav - en so bright;

My gra - cious Re - deem - er, my Sav - iour art thou,
I love thee for wear - ing the thorns on thy brow;
And say, when the death - dew lies cold on my brow,
I'll sing with the glit - ter - ing crown on my brow,

If ev - er I loved thee, my Je - sus, 'tis now.

Cast thy Burden on the Lord.

"Casting all your care upon him, for he careth for you."
1 Peter v. 7.

W. J. K.   Wm. J. Kirkpatrick.

1. Wea-ry pil-grim on life's pathway, Struggling on beneath thy load,
2. Are thy tir-ed feet unstead-y? Does thy lamp no light af-ford?
3. Are the ties of friendship severed? Hushed the voices fond-ly heard?

Hear these words of con-so-la-tion,—"Cast thy bur-den on the Lord."
Is thy cross too great and hea-vy? Cast thy bur-den on the Lord.
Breaks thy heart with weight of anguish, Cast thy bur-den on the Lord.

CHORUS.

Cast thy bur-den on the Lord, Cast thy bur-den on the Lord, And he will

strengthen thee, sustain and comfort thee; Cast thy bur-den on the Lord.

4 Does thy heart with faintness falter?
  Does thy mind forget his word?
  Does thy strength succumb to weak-
  Cast thy burden on the Lord. [ness?

5 He will hold thee up from falling,
  He will guide thy steps aright;
  He will strengthen each endeavor;
  He will keep thee by his might.

Saved to the Uttermost.

W. J. K.

WM. J. KIRKPATRICK.

1. Saved to the uttermost: I am the Lord's, Jesus my Saviour salvation affords,
2. Saved to the uttermost: Jesus is near, Keeping me safely, he casteth out fear:
3. Saved to the uttermost: this I can say,"Once all was darkness,but now it is day,"
4. Saved to the uttermost: cheerfully sing Loud hallelujahs to Jesus, my King

Gives me his Spirit a witness within, Whisp'ring of pardon,and saving from sin.
Trusting his promises,how I am blest! Leaning upon him, how sweet is my rest!
Beauti- ful vis- ions of glo- ry I see, Je- sus in brightness revealed unto me.
Ransom'd and pardon'd,redeemed by his blood,Cleansed from unrighteousness,glory
[to God!

CHORUS.

Saved, saved, saved to the uttermost, Saved, saved by pow- er di- vine;

Saved, saved, saved to the uttermost, Je - sus the Saviour is mine.

From "Precious Songs," by per.

God be with You.

"The grace of our Lord Jesus Christ be with you."
Rom. xvi. 20.

J. E. Rankin, D. D.   W. G. Tomer.

1. God be with you till we meet again, By his counsels guide, uphold you,
2. God be with you till we meet again, 'Neath his wings securely hide you;
3. God be with you till we meet again, When life's perils thick confound you;
4. God be with you till we meet again, Keep love's banner floating o'er you;

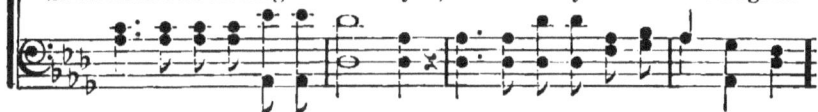

With his sheep securely fold you, God be with you till we meet again.
Dai - ly manna still provide you, God be with you till we meet again.
Put his arms unfailing round you, God be with you till we meet again.
Smite death's threat'ning wave before you, God be with you till we meet again.

CHORUS.

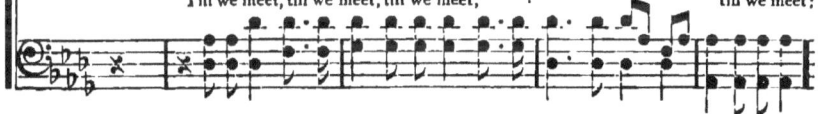

Till we meet,   till we meet,   Till we meet at Je - sus' feet;
Till we meet, till we meet, till we meet,   till we meet;

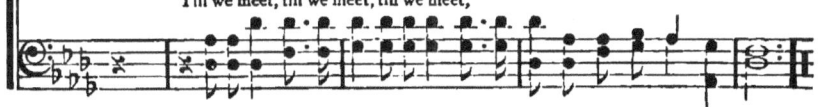

Till we meet,   till we meet,   God be with you till we meet again.
Till we meet, till we meet, till we meet,

Christ is All.

"Unto you therefore which believe he is precious." W. A. WILLIAMS.

Effective as a Solo. *Ad lib.* 1 Peter ii. 7.

1. I entered once a home of care, For age and pen - u - ry were there,
2. I stood beside a dy-ing bed, Where lay a child with aching head,
3. I saw the mar - tyr at the stake, The flames could not his courage shake,
4. I saw the gos - pel her-ald go,— To Afric's sand and Greenland's snow,

Yet peace and joy withal; I asked the lonely mother whence Her helpless
Wait-ing for Jesus' call; I marked his smile,'twas sweet as May, And as his
Nor death his soul appal, I asked him whence his strength was given, He looked tri-
To save from Satan's thrall, Nor home nor life he counted dear,'Midst wants and

CHORUS.

widowhood's defense, She told me "Christ was all." Christ is all, all in
spir - it passed a-way, He whispered, "Christ is all."
umphant-ly to heaven, And answered, "Christ is all."
per - ils owned no fear, He felt that "Christ is all."

1st time. *2d time.*

all, Yes, Christ is all in all: Yes, Christ is all in all.

5 I dreamed that hoary time had fled,
And earth and sea gave up their dead,
A fire dissolved this ball,
I saw the church's ransomed throng,
I heard the burden of their song,
'Twas "Christ is all in all."

6 Then come to Christ, oh, come to-day,
The Father, Son, and Spirit say;
The Bride repeats the call,
For he will cleanse your guilty stains,
His love will soothe your weary pains,
For "Christ is all in all."

By permission

Delay Not to Come.

E. A. HOFFMAN.   JNO. R. SWENEY. By per.

1. De - lay not to come to Christ! The moments are fleet - ing
2. De - lay not to come to Christ! Thy heart will grow hard as
3. De - lay not to come to Christ! For soon it may be too

on,   And   ere thou art   scarce a - ware,   The
steel,   Un - til, tho' the   Sav - iour   calls,   Thy
late,   And   thou may'st be   left in   sin,   Un -

CHORUS.

day of thy life may be   gone.)   De - lay . . . .   not to
spir - it no long - er can   feel. }   De - lay not, de - lay not, O
pardoned at sweet mercy's   gate.)   De - lay not, de - lay not, O

come, . . . De - lay . . . . not to come, . . . While
sinner, to come, De - lay not, de - lay not, O sin - ner, to come, For

Je - - - sus in - vites, . . . Delay not, delay not to   come.
Jesus hath power to save thee this hour, Oh, delay not, delay not to   come.

Sunshine in the Soul.

E. E. Hewitt.   Jno. R. Sweney.

1. There's sunshine in my soul to-day, More glo-ri-ous and bright Than
2. There's mu-sic in my soul to-day, A car-ol to my King, And
3. There's springtime in my soul to-day, For when the Lord is near The
4. There's gladness in my soul to-day, And hope, and praise, and love, For

REFRAIN.

glows in an-y earthly sky, For Je-sus is my light. Oh, there's
Je-sus, list-ening, can hear The songs I can-not sing.
dove of peace sings in my heart, The flowers of grace ap-pear.
blessings which he gives me now, For joys "laid up" a-bove.

sun - - shine, blessed sun - shine, When the peaceful, happy moments
sunshine in the soul, bless-ed sunshine in the soul,

roll;   When Jesus shows his smiling face There is sunshine in the soul.
happy moments roll;

Breathe upon Us.

Mrs. R. N. Turner, Alt.

Wm. J. Kirkpatrick.

1. Re - vive, O Lord, our waiting souls, Re-new our al - tar fire!
2. Help us to con - se-crate ourselves A - new to thy dear will;
3. O, light the fires of fer - vid love Within each breast to - day,
4. Im - bue us with thy Spir - it, Lord, And pu - ri - fy each heart.

And ev - 'ry heart, for thy blest work, With sa-cred zeal in - spire!
With liv - ing words and earnest deeds Thy bless-ed law ful - fill!
And draw us clos - er now to thee, And bless us while we pray.
Bap - tize us with the pow'r we need ; New life and strength im - part!

REFRAIN.

Come, Lord, and breathe upon us, With thine own soul di - vine,

And o'er thy waiting church below In strength and glo - ry shine!

156 Beautiful Robes.

E. E. HEWITT.   WM. J. KIRKPATRICK.

Not too fast.

1. We shall walk with him in white, In that country pure and bright, Where shall
2. We shall walk with him in white, Where faith yields to blissful sight, When the
3. We shall walk with him in white, By the fountains of delight, Where the

enter naught that may defile; Where the day-beam ne'er declines, For the
beauty of the King we see; Holding converse full and sweet, In a
Lamb his ransomed ones shall lead, For his blood shall wash each stain, Till no

blessed light that shines Is the glo - ry of the Saviour's smile.
fel - lowship complete; Waking songs of ho - ly mel - o - dy.
spot of sin remain, And the soul for - ev - ermore is freed.

CHORUS.

Beau - - tiful robes, . . Beau - - tiful robes, . .
Beautiful robes, beautiful robes, Beautiful robes, beautiful robes,

Beau - - - ti - ful robes we then shall wear, . .
Beau - ti - ful robes we then shall wear, Beau - ti - ful robes we then shall wear,

Gar - - ments of light, . . . Love - - ly and bright, . .
Garments of light, . . Garments of light, Lovely and bright, . . Lovely and bright,

Walking with Je - sus in white, Beau-ti - ful robes we shall wear.

The Golden Key.

"Prayer is the key to unlock the door, and the bolt to shut in the night."

JNO. R. SWENEY.

1. Prayer is the key For the bending knee To open the morn's first hours;
2. Not a soul so sad, Nor a heart so glad, When cometh the shades of night,
3. Take the golden key In your hand and see, As the night tide drifts away,

See the incense rise To the starry skies, Like per-fume from the flow'rs.
But the daybreak song Will the joy prolong, And some darkness turn to light.
How its blessed hold Is a crown of gold, Thro' the weary hours of day.

4 When the shadows fall,
And the vesper call
Is sobbing its low refrain,
'Tis a garland sweet
To the toil dent feet,
And an antidote for pain

5 Soon the year's dark door
Shall be shut no more:
Life's tears shall be wiped away,
As the pearl gates swing,
And the gold harps ring,
And the sun unsheathe for aye.

The Haven of Rest.

H. L. GILMOUR.　　　　　　　　　　　　　　　　　　　　GEO. D. MOORE.

1. My soul in sad ex - ile was out on life's sea, So
2. I yield - ed my - self to his ten - der embrace, And
3. The song of my soul, since the Lord made me whole, Has
4. How pre - cious the thought that we all may re - cline, Like
5. Oh, come to the Sav - iour, he pa - tient-ly waits To

burdened with sin, and dis - trest, Till I heard a sweet voice saying,
faith taking hold of the word, My fetters fell off, and I
been the OLD STORY so blest, Of Jesus, who'll save who-so-
John the be- lov - ed and blest, On Jesus' strong arm, where no
save by his power di - vine; Come, anchor your soul in the

D. S.—The tempest may sweep o'er the

Fine.

make me your choice; And I entered the "Ha - ven of Rest!"
anchored my soul; The ha - ven of rest is my Lord.
ev - er will have A home in the "Ha - ven of Rest!"
tem - pest can harm,— Se - cure in the "Ha - ven of Rest!"
ha - ven of rest, And say, "my Be - lov - ed is mine."

wild, stormy deep, In Je - sus I'm safe ev - er - more.

CHORUS.　　　　　　　　　　　　　　　　　　　　*D. S.*

I've anchored my soul in the haven of rest, I'll sail the wide seas no more;

Home of the Soul.

Mrs. Ellen H. Gates.

Philip Phillips. By per.

1. I will sing you a song of that beau - ti - ful land,
2. Oh, that home of the soul in my vis - ions and dreams,
3. That un - chang - a - ble home is for you and for me,
4. Oh, how sweet it will be in that beau - ti - ful land,

The far a- way home of the soul, Where no storms ev - er
Its bright, jas- per walls I can see; Till I fan - cy but
Where Je - sus of Naz - ar - eth stands; The King of all
So free from all sor - row and pain; With songs on our

beat on the glit - tering strand, While the years of e - ter - ni - ty
thin - ly the vail in - tervenes Be - tween the fair cit - y and
kingdoms for - ev - er is he, And he hold- eth our crowns in his
lips, and with harps in our hands, To meet one an - oth - er a

roll, While the years of e - ter - ni - ty roll; ter - ni - ty roll.
me, Be - tween the fair ci - ty and me; ci - ty and me.
hands, And he holdeth our crowns in his hands; crowns in his hands.
gain, To meet one an - oth - er a - gain; oth - er a - gain.

160 His Blood Washes Whiter than Snow.

JOSHUA GILL.　　　　　　　　　　　　　　　　　　　　　JNO. R. SWENEY.

1. Je - sus saves me and keeps me from sin, By the blood that he shed on the
2. It is bless-ed his presence to feel, And his faithful dis-ci-ple to
3. In his care I am hap-py and blest, And his perfect peace flows unto
4. When in glo-ry the Saviour we meet, When the King in his beauty we

tree; Through his Spir-it and Word I am clean, For his grace is a-
be; For his love he delights to re-veal, And his grace is a-
me, And my spir-it is al-ways at rest, For his grace is a-
see, We'll con-fess, as we fall at his feet, That his grace is a-

REFRAIN.

bundant and free. I be-lieve Je-sus saves, And his
　　　　　　　　　　　I believe Je-sus saves,

blood wash-es whit-er than snow, I be-lieve
　　　　　　　　　　Yes, whit-er than snow, I be-lieve Je-sus saves,

Je-sus saves, And his blood washes whit-er than snow.
I be-lieve Je-sus saves.

WM. H. CLARK.   W. J. KIRKPATRICK.

1. I'm help-less, Lord, to thee I fly, In mer-cy hear me
2. I know thou wilt my sins for-give, For thou hast bid me
3. My Sav-iour now is lift-ed up, I look to him, my
4. And now I hear thy pard'ning voice, That bids me in thy

when I cry, While now I urge one on-ly plea:
turn and live, With long-ing heart I come to thee;
on-ly hope, I trust thy word, and press the plea:
love re-joice, My soul doth tri-umph in the plea:

CHORUS.

Je-sus of Naz-a-reth died for me! Je-sus of Naz-a-reth died for me,

Died to re-deem me and set me free; This is my hope, my

on-ly plea: Je-sus of Naz-a-reth died for me!

Jesus is Precious to Me

"Unto you therefore which believe he is precious." 1 Peter, ii. 7.

PRISCILLA J. OWENS.　　　　　　　　　　　　　　　　　W. J. KIRKPATRICK.

1. Sweet is the name of my Lord, Hap-py his servants must be,
2. Precious his love that sus-tains, Precious in joy and de-light,
3. Precious in days of my youth, Precious in age and de-cline,
4. Precious the blood that he shed, Precious the tears that he wept,
5. Precious the cross that I bear, Sent as a to-ken of love,

Singing in joy-ful ac-cord, "Je-sus is precious to me."
Precious in conflict and pains, Precious in sor-row and night.
Precious the voice of his truth, Precious the hope that is mine.
Precious the ransom he paid, Precious the grave where he slept.
Precious the crown I shall wear, Radiant with glo-ry a-bove.

CHORUS.

Je-sus is precious to me, . . Je-sus is precious to me, . .
to me,　　　　　　　　　　　　　　　　　　　to me.

Saved by his grace, so full, so free, Je-sus is precious to me. . . .
to me.

Take hold, hold on.

Advice of an aged colored man to young converts, "Take hold, hold on, hold fast and never let go!"

PRISCILLA J. OWENS.   WM. J. KIRKPATRICK.

1. O, turn not back in the Christian race Till the prize is won we know;
2. O, turn not back on life's battle-field, Tho' the world's a mighty foe,
3. Truth's anchor firm-ly,   sure-ly clasp, As the billows near thee flow,
4. Though danger threatens or death alarms, In each ris-ing flood of woe,

Reach up to Christ for abounding grace, Take hold and nev-er let go!
God's arms are round thee   as a shield, Take hold and nev-er let go!
God's hand will close o'er thy feeble grasp, Take hold and nev-er let go!
Still cling to God's ev-er-last-ing arms, Take hold and nev-er let go!

CHORUS.

Take hold,   hold on,   Hold fast and nev-er let   go!   No
Take hold,   hold on,   hold on!

matter how the wind in the tempest may blow, Take hold and never let go!

164 Praise the Lord for His Love to Me.

Henrietta E. Blair. (Sing also "O how Happy are They.") Wm. J. Kirkpatrick.

1. On the cold, bar-ren hills I had wan-dered a - far,— I was
2. Oh, the depths of his love that my sin could re-move, When so
3. Oh, the joy that I feel I can nev - er re - veal, There is
4. Praise the Lord, O my soul, for the work he has done, For his

wea - ry, as wea - ry could be,—When the kind, lov-ing voice of the
long I had turned from his call, But my guilt I confessed, for my
light where my pathway was dim ; I was lost till he came, now by
good - ness and mer - cy to me, For the hope of a rest in the

REFRAIN.

Saviour I heard, And I knew he was seeking for me. Praise the
heart was oppressed, And he free - ly for-gave me for all.
faith in his name I am trust-ing my fu - ture to him.
land of the blest, Where for - ev - er with him I shall be.

Lord, praise the Lord, O my soul, rejoice and sing ; Praise the Lord for his love to me,
[He re-

[Lord.

deemed me with his blood, O, the precious, cleansing flood. Hallelujah, praise the

He Saves to the Uttermost.

CHAS. J. BUTLER.   JNO. R. SWENEY.

1. I was once far a-way from the Sav-iour, And as vile as a
2. But there in that lone-ly hour A voice sweet-ly
3. I then ful-ly trust-ed in Je-sus, And oh, what a

sin-ner could be; I won-der'd if Christ, the Re-deem-er
whisper'd to me, Saying, "Christ, the Redeem-er, hath pow-er
joy came to me! My heart was filled with his prais-es,

Would save a poor sinner like me. I wan-der'd on in the
To save a poor sinner like thee." I listen'd, and lo! 'twas the
For he sav'd a poor sinner like me. No long-er in darkness I'm

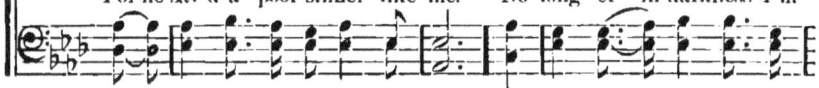

dark-ness, Not a ray of light could I see; And the
Sav-iour That was speak-ing so kind to me; I
walk-ing, For the light is shin-ing on me; And

thought fill'd my heart with sad-ness, There's no hope for a sinner like me.
cried, "I'm the chief of sinners, Thou cans't save a poor sinner like me.
now un-to oth-ers I'm tell-ing How he sav'd a poor sinner like me.

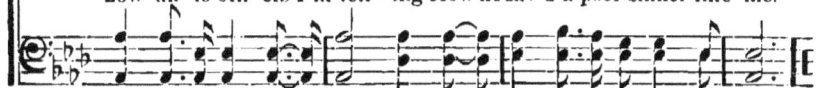

In the Morning.

LIZZIE EDWARDS.　　　　　　　　　　　　　　　　JNO. R. SWENEY.

1. We are pilgrims looking home, Sad and wea-ry oft we roam, But we
2. O these tender broken ties, How they dim our aching eyes, But like
3. When our fettered souls are free, Far beyond the narrow sea, And we
4. Thro' our pilgrim journey here, Tho' the night is sometimes drear, Let us

know 'twill all be well in the morning; When, our anchor firmly cast, Ev'ry
jewels they will shine in the morning; When our victor palms we bear, And our
hear the Saviour's voice in the morning; When our golden sheaves we bring To the
watch and persevere till the morning; Then our highest tribute raise For the

storm-y wave is past, And we gather safe at last in the morn-ing.
robes immor-tal wear, We shall know each other there, in the morn-ing.
feet of Christ our King, What a chorus we shall sing in the morn-ing.
love that crowns our days, And to Jesus give the praise in the morn-ing.

D. S.—sun-ny region bright, When we hail the blessed light of the morn-ing.

CHORUS.

When we all meet a-gain in the morn-ing, On the sweet blooming

hills in the morn-ing; Nev-ermore to say good night In that

Help Just a Little.

Music from " The Wells of Salvation,"
new words by Rev. W. A. SPENCER.

WM. J. KIRKPATRICK.

1. Brother for Christ's kingdom sighing, Help a lit-tle, help a lit-tle;
2. Is thy cup made sad by tri-al? Help a lit-tle, help a lit-tle;
3. Though no wealth to thee is giv-en, Help a lit-tle, help a lit-tle;

Help to save the mil-lions dy-ing, Help just a lit-tle.
Sweet-en it with self-de-ni-al, Help just a lit-tle.
Sac-ri-fice is gold in heav-en, Help just a lit-tle.

CHORUS.

Oh, the wrongs that we may righten! Oh, the hearts that we may lighten!

Oh, the skies that we may brighten! Helping just a lit-tle.

4 Let us live for one another,
  Help a little, help a little;
Help to lift each fallen brother,
  Help just a little.

5 Tho' thy life is pressed with sorrow,
  Help a little, help a little;
Bravely look t'ward God's to-morrow,
  Help just a little.

Leaning on Jesus.

Rev. W. F. Crafts.   Wm. J. Kirkpatrick.

1. Wea-ry with walking a - lone, Long heav-y - laden with sin;
2. Fearing to stand for my Lord, Trembling for weakness in prayer;

Toil-ing all night with-out Christ,—Rest for my soul shall I win,
Yet on the bo-som di - vine Los - ing each sor-row and fear,

CHORUS.

Lean - ing on Je - sus, I walk - at his side; . .
Leaning on Je-sus, in him I a - bide.   Leaning on Je - sus, I walk at his side;

Lean - - ing on Je - - sus, I trust him, my Shepherd and Guide.
Leaning on Je- sus, what-ev- er be - tide,

3 Anxious no longer for self,
   Shrinking no longer from pain,
  Leaning on Jesus alone,
   He all my care will sustain.

4 Leaning, I walk in "the way,"
   Leaning, " the truth " I shall know;
  Leaning on heart-throbs of Christ,
   Safe into " life " I may go.

From " Leaflet Gems," by permission of John J. Hood.

Trusting in the Promise.

Rev. H. B. HARTZLER.

E. S. LORENZ.

1. {
I have found repose for my weary soul,
And a harbor safe when the billows roll,
} Trusting in the promise of the Saviour;

2. {
I will sing my song as the days go by,
And rejoice in hope, while I live or die,
} Trusting in the promise of the Saviour;

3. {
O the peace and joy of the life I live,
O the strength and love only God can give,
} Trusting in the promise of the Saviour;

{
I will fear no foe in the deadly strife,
I will bear my lot in the toil of life,
} Trusting in the promise of the Saviour;

{
I can smile at grief, and abide in pain,
And the loss of all shall be highest gain,
} Trusting in the promise of the Saviour;

{
Whosoever will may be saved to-day,
And begin to walk in the holy way,
} Trusting in the promise of the Saviour;

REFRAIN.

Resting on his mighty arm forev-er, Never from his loving heart to sever,

I will rest by grace in his strong embrace, Trusting in the promise of the Saviour;

From "Songs of Refreshing," by per.

Beautiful Christmas.

Mrs. M. B. C. Slade.　　　　　　　　　　R. M. McIntosh.　By per.

1. O'er the hills and a - down the snow-y dells, As the
2. Bring good - will to the suf - fer - ing and sad; Speak the
3. Peace on earth! bid all strife and tu - mult cease: For this
4. So glad hearts on this hap - py Christmas night Bring your

ech - oes ring of the Christmas bells, An - gel songs in our
ten - der word that shall make them glad: Tell them how, o'er the
night a - gain gives the Lord his peace, While our hands shall his
gifts of love, make his al - tar bright, Sing glad songs that shall

FINE.

hearts resound a - gain, Sing-ing peace on earth and good-will to men!
hills of Beth - le - hem When the an-gels sang, 'twas good news for them.
tem - ple beau - ti - fy, Car - ol, glo - ry be un - to God most high.
sweet-ly sound as when An - gels sang of peace and good-will to men.

CHORUS.

Bring pine and fir - tree, weave the gar - lands bright;

Glad - den the tem - ple of the King to-night! Christmas is here!

D.C.

Fill it with cheer; Make it glo-ri-ous with joy and light.

I am Saved.

Mrs. S. L. Oberholtzer.

Jno. R. Sweney. By per.

1. I am sav'd! the Lord hath sav'd me, Help me shout the glorious news!
2. Loud I sing my ex-ul-ta-tion, Hoping it will reach the skies,
3. Free sal-va-tion! glad salva-tion! Let us shout from pole to pole,
4. When at last the days are gathered In-to thy great judgment one,

I have tast-ed God's salva-tion, And 'tis sweet as honeyed dews.
Keep, dear Lord, my soul forev-er Un-der thy pro-tect-ing eyes,
Un-til each dis-eased na-tion Feels that God hath made it whole.
May I find my name deep written In the re-cords of thy Son.

CHORUS.

Glo-ry, glo-ry, hal-le-lu-jah! I re-joice sal-va-tion came;

Glo-ry, glo-ry, hal-le-lu-jah! I am saved in Je-sus, name.

"For the Lord thy God bringeth thee into a good land, a land of brooks of water, of fountains, and depths that spring out of valleys and hills." "And I will give her the valley of "BEULAH."   Achor for a door of hope: and she shall sing there."   GRACE WEISER.

1. God has given me a song, a song of trust, song of trust, And I sing it all day
2. O, I sing it on the mountain, in the light,   Where the radiance of God's
3. And I sing it in the valley dark and low, When my heart is crush'd with
4. When I sing it in the desert parched and dry,   Living streams begin to

5. For I've crossed the river Jordan, and I stand   In the blessed land of

long, for sing I must; sing I must; Ev-'ry hour it sweeter grows, Fills my
sunshine makes all bright;   All my path seems bright and clear, Heav'nly
sor-row, pain, and woe;   Then the shadows flee a-way, Like the
flow, a rich supply;   Verdure in abundance grows, Deserts

promise,—Beulah land: Trusting is like breathing here, Just as

soul with blest re-pose, Just how rest-ful no one knows but those who trust.
land seems very near: Why, I almost then appear to walk by sight.
night when dawns the day; Trust in God brings light alway, I find it so.
blossom like a rose, And my heart with joy o'erflows at God's reply.

easy,—doubt and fear Van-ish in this at-mosphere, in Beu-lah land.

CHORUS.

Ye who trust in the Lord, Oh, sing a glad refrain; Raise your songs on high, His mighty love pro-claim; For his prom-ise is sure, Ye shall

not be put to shame, Ye shall never be confounded again: Praise his name!

Surrendered.

H. L. G.   Dr. H. L. Gilmour.

1. I have surren-dered to the Lord, The world no long-er pleas-es;
2. How ten-der-ly he holds my hand! Thro' pastures green he leads me;
3. By day by night he's always near, Sweet joy and comfort bringing;

I'm yielding all to his control, Ac-cept-ing on-ly Je-sus.
My thirsting soul he sat-is-fies, With heavenly man-na feeds me.
Oh, how my soul ex-ults a-new When praise to Je-sus sing-ing.

4 No noonday drought affects my soul,
   In Jesus I'm confiding;
Oh, constant, sweet companionship,
   With Christ in me abiding.

5 Oh, victory that's always sure!
   Oh, blest emancipation!
Oh, vanquished tempter of my soul!
   Oh, free and full salvation!

From "Melodious Sonnets," by per.

Are You Drifting?

Mary D. James.

Wm. J. Kirkpatrick.

1. Are you drifting down life's current, Drift-ing on a dang'rous tide?
2. Down the stream of worldly pleasure Drift-ing, drifting ev - er- more
3. Heed, oh, heed the kind moni - tion! Give your aimless wand'rings o'er;

Near the rapids' fearful per - il All unconscious do ye glide?
T'ward the great unfathomed o - cean, Bound for yon e - ter-nal shore?
Cease to seek in earth your pleasure, Head your bark for heav'n's bright shore,

Down the stream of sin and fol - ly,—Heed-ing not the danger near,
Drift - ing, drifting,—going,—whither? Aim - less, purposeless;—how vain!
Take on board the skillful pi - lot, Use the oars of faith and prayer;

Drift - ing on in self-com- pla - cence, Feel - ing no remorse or fear?
To the dark and dread forev - er! What, oh, what have ye to gain?
Then you'll make the port of glo - ry, God will guide you safely there.

CHORUS.

Hark the voice . . of yonder pilot: Cease your drifting, seize the oar;

Hark the voice, the warning voice of yonder pilot: seize the oar;

Make the blest, celestial harbor, Steer your bark for Canaan's shore.

Make the blest, celestial harbor, make the harbor,

Give me Jesus.

Arr. by W. J. K.

1. When I'm hap-py, hear me sing, When I'm happy, hear me sing, When I'm
2. When in sor-row, hear me pray, When in sorrow, hear me pray, When in
3. When I'm dy-ing, hear me cry, When I'm dying, hear me cry, When I'm
4. When I'm ris-ing, hear me shout, When I'm rising, hear me shout, When I'm
5. When in heav-en, we will sing, When in heav-en, we will sing, When in

CHORUS.

hap-py, hear me sing, Give me Je - sus, Give me Je - sus, Give me
sorrow, hear me pray, Give me Je - sus,
dying, hear me cry, Give me Je - sus,
rising, hear me shout, Give me Je - sus,
heaven, we will sing, Blessed Je - sus, Bles-sed Je - sus, Bles-sed

Je - sus; You may have all the world: Give me Je - sus.
Je - sus, By thy grace we are saved, Bles-sed Je - sus.

He will Gather the Wheat.

Harriet B. M'Keever.   Jno. R. Sweney.

1. When Je- sus shall gather the na - tions Be- fore him at last to ap- pear,
2. Shall we hear, from the lips of the Saviour, The words, ' Faithful servant, well done;'
3. He will smile when he looks on his children, And sees on the ransomed his seal;

Then how shall we stand in the judgment, When summoned our sentence to hear?
Or, trembling with fear and with anguish, Be banished away from his throne?
He will clothe them in heavenly beau - ty, As low at his footstool they kneel,

CHORUS.

He will gather the wheat in his gar - ner, But the chaff will he scatter a-way;

Then how shall we stand in the judgment, Oh, how shall it be in that day?

4 Then let us be watching and waiting,—
Our lamps burning steady and bright,—
When the Bridegroom shall call to the wed-
Our spirits made ready for flight. [ding

5 Thus living with hearts fixed on Jesus.
In patience we wait for the time,
When, the days of our pilgrimage ended,
We'll bask in his presence divine

Jesus will Forgive.

Mrs. Loula K. Rogers. R. M. McIntosh. By per.

1. Come, ye sin-ners, come to-day: Je-sus will forgive you free-ly.
2. Come un-to the mer-cy-seat: Je-sus will forgive you free-ly.

All your sins he'll wash a-way: Je-sus will forgive you free-ly.
Hum-bly fall-ing at his feet: Je-sus will forgive you free-ly.

REFRAIN.

O, come to-day! Why lon-ger stay a-way? He will not

say you nay: Je-sus will for-give you free-ly.

3. Lay your treasures up above :
   Jesus will forgive you freely.
   Trust the riches of his love :
   Jesus will forgive you freely.

4. Earnestly a blessing seek :
   Jesus will forgive you freely.
   Trembling sinner, faint and weak,
   Jesus will forgive you freely.

5. He is able all to save :
   Jesus will forgive you freely.
   For your love his blood he gave :
   Jesus will forgive you freely.

6. Then, ye sinners, come to-day :
   Jesus will forgive you freely.
   All your sins he'll wash away :
   Jesus will forgive you freely.

Beulah Land.

EDGAR PAGE. *"He shall give thee the desires of thine heart."* JNO. R. SWENEY.

1. I've reached the land of corn and wine, And all its rich-es free-ly mine;
2. My Saviour comes and walks with me, And sweet communion here have we;
3. A sweet perfume up - on the breeze Is borne from ev-er - ver- nal trees,
4. The zephyrs seem to float to me Sweet sounds of heaven's mel- o - dy,

Here shines undimm'd one blissful day, For all my night has pass'd a - way.
He gen- tly leads me by his hand, For this is heav- en's border - land.
And flowers, that never- fad- ing grow Where streams of life for- ev - er flow.
As angels with the white-robed throng Join in the sweet re - demption song.

CHORUS.

O Beu-lah Land, sweet Beulah Land, As on thy high- est mount I stand,

I look a - way a - cross the sea, Where mansions are pre-pared for me,

And view the shin- ing glo-ry shore,—My heav'n, my home, for ev - er-more!

From " Goodly Pearls," by per.

He Hideth my Soul.

FANNY J. CROSBY.   WM. J. KIRKPATRICK.

Allegretto.

1. A wonderful Saviour is Je- sus my Lord, A wonderful Saviour to
2. A wonderful Saviour is Je- sus my Lord, He taketh my burden a -
3. With numberless blessings each moment he crowns, And fill'd with his fulness di-
4. When clothed in his brightness transported I rise To meet him in clouds of the

me,   He hideth my soul in the cleft of the rock, Where rivers of
way,   He holdeth me up, and I shall not be moved, He giveth me
vine,   I sing in my rapture, oh, glo - ry to God For such a Re-
sky,   His perfect salvation, his wonderful love, I'll shout with the

CHORUS.

pleasure I see.   He hideth my soul in the cleft of the rock, That
strength as my day.
deemer as mine!
millions on high.

shadows a dry, thirsty land; He hid- eth my life in the depths of his

love, And covers me there with his hand, And covers me there with his hand.

180 I Hope to Meet You All in Glory.

EMMA PITT. [From "Our Sabbath Home," by per.] WM. J. KIRKPATRICK.

1. I hope to meet you all in glo - ry, When the storms of life are o'er;
2. I hope to meet you all in glo - ry, By the tree of life so fair;
3. I hope to meet you all in glo - ry, Round the Saviour's throne above:
4. I hope to meet you all in glo - ry, When my work on earth is o'er;

I hope to tell the dear old sto - ry, On the bles-sed shin-ing shore.
I hope to praise our dear Redeem-er For the grace that brought me there.
I hope to join the ransomed arm - y Singing now redeem-ing love.
I hope to clasp your hands rejoic-ing On the bright e - ter - nal shore.

CHORUS.

On the shin - ing shore, On the gold - en strand, In our

Father's home, In the hap - py land: I hope to meet you there, I

hope to meet you there,—A crown of vict-'ry wear,—In glo - ry.

Trusting in Jesus.

FRANK GOULD.   JNO. R. SWENEY.

1. Trusting in Jesus, my Saviour divine, I have the witness that still he is mine;
2. Once I was far from my Saviour and King, Now he has taught me his mercy to sing;
3. Trusting in Jesus, oh, what should I fear? Nothing can harm me when he is so near!
4. If while a stranger I journey below Filled with his fulness such rapture I know,

Great are the blessings he giveth to me: Oh, I am happy as mortal can be.
Peace in believing he giveth to me: Oh, I am happy as mortal can be.
Sweet is the promise he giveth to me: Oh, I am happy as mortal can be.
What will the bliss of eter-ni-ty be, When in his beauty the King I shall see?

CHORUS.

I am re-deemed, and I know it full well, full well, Saved by his grace, I with him shall dwell; Saved by his grace I am re-deemed, and the shall dwell; child of his love, his love, Heir to a glo - - rious crown a-bove. above.

182 When the Mists have Cleared Away.

ANNIE HERBERT.　　　　　　　　　　　　　　　　　R. M. McINTOSH.　By per.

1. When the mists have rolled in splendor From the sum - mit of the
2. If we err in hu-man blindness, And for - get that we are
3. When the mists shall rise a - bove us, As our Fa - ther knows his

hills,　　And the sun-shine, warm and ten - der, Falls in
dust;　　If we miss the law of kind - ness, When we
own,　　Face to face with those that love us, We shall

beau - ty on the rills, We may read love's shining let - ter
strug - gle to be just, Snowy wings of love shall cov - er
know as we are known; Lo! be-yond the o-ri-ent meadows

In the rain - bow of the spray; We shall know each oth - er
All the faults that cloud our day, When the wea - ry watch is
Floats the gold - en fringe of day; Heart to heart, we bide the

bet - ter, When the mists have clear'd a - way.
o - ver, And the mists have clear'd a - way.　　We shall
shad - ows Till the mists have clear'd a - way.

know . . . as we are known, . . . Nev-er
We shall know as we are known,

more . . . to walk a-lone; . . . . In the
Nev - er more to walk a - lone; In the

dawn - ing of the morning, When the mists . . . have
In the dawning have clear'd away,

cleared a - way; In the dawn - - ing of the
In the dawn-ing

morn-ing, When the mists . . . . have clear'd a - way.
have clear'd away,

184 **His Anger is Turned Away.**

F. G. Burroughs.   Psalm 30. 5.   H. L. Gilmour.

1. O Lord, I will praise thee, For though thou wast angry, Thine anger is
2. O Lord, I will praise thee, Because thou hast saved me, And welcomed thy
3. O Lord, I will praise thee, For great is thy mercy, To par-don trans-
4. O Lord, I will praise thee, For though thou wast angry, Thine anger is

turned away! By grace now is pardoned This heart that was hardened; From
prodigal home; Thy great love abiding Hath healed my back sliding; From
gressions like mine: Tho' summer had ended, Thine angels defend-ed, And
turned a - way! Thy comforts now cheer me, Thy presence is near me, Thou

CHORUS.

sin I am ransomed to - day.   Ho- san - na! ho-san - na! The
thee I will nev - er more roam.
kept this late tro - phy of thine.
lov - est me free - ly to - day!

Lord is my banner, His an - ger is turned a - way! My chains have been

riv - en. My sins all for - given; O Lord, I will praise thee to - day.

Welcome for Me.

Fanny J. Crosby.

Wm. J. Kirkpatrick.

1. Like a bird on the deep, far a-way from its nest, I had
2. I am safe in the ark; I have fold-ed my wings On the
3. I am safe in the ark, and I dread not the storm, Though a-

wandered, my Saviour, from thee; But thy dear lov-ing voice called me
bo-som of mer-cy di - vine; I am filled with the light of thy
round me the surg-es may roll; I will look to the skies, where the

home to thy breast, And I knew there was wel-come for me.
pres-ence so bright, And the joy that will ev - er be mine.
day nev-er dies, I will sing of the joy in my soul.

CHORUS.

Welcome for me, Saviour, from thee; A smile and a welcome for me:

Now, like a dove, I rest in thy love, And find a sweet refuge in thee. in thee.

Abiding in Him.

Chas. B. J. Root.   Melody by D. C. Wright, arranged

1. A-bid-ing, oh, so wondrous sweet! I'm resting at the Saviour's feet;
2. He speaks, and by his word is given His peace, a rich foretaste of heaven!
3. I live; not I; thro' him alone By whom the mighty work is done:—
4. Now rest, my heart, the work is done, I'm saved thro' the Eter - nal Son!

I trust in him, I'm sat - is-fied, I'm rest-ing in the Cru - ci-fied!
Not as the world he peace doth give, 'Tis thro' this hope my soul shall live.
Dead to myself, a - live to him, I count all loss his rest to gain.
Let all my powers my soul employ, To tell the world my peace and joy.

CHORUS.

A - bid - ing, a - bid - ing, Oh! so wondrous sweet!
A - bid - ing in him, I'm rest-ing in him, Oh! so wondrous sweet, wondrous sweet!

I'm rest - ing, rest - ing At the Saviour's feet.
I'm rest-ing in him, rest-ing in him, At the Sav - iour's feet, at his feet.

FANNY J. CROSBY. Wm. J. KIRKPATRICK.

1. Watch and pray that when the Master cometh, If at morning, noon or night,
2. Watch and pray; the tempter may be near us; Keep the heart with jealous care,
3. Watch and pray, nor let us ev- er wea- ry; Jesus watched and prayed alone;
4. Watch and pray, nor leave our post of duty, Till we hear the Bridegroom's voice:

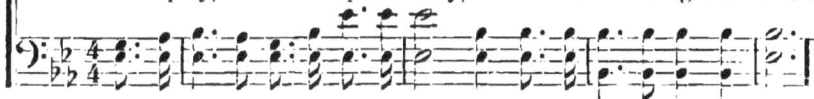

He may find a lamp in ev'ry window, Trimmed and burning clear and bright.
Lest the door, a moment left unguard - ed Evil thoughts may enter there.
Prayed for us when on- ly stars beheld him, While on Olive's brow they shone.
Then, with him the marriage feast partaking, We shall ev - ermore re - joice.

CHORUS.

Watch and pray, ... the Lord command - - - eth; Watch and
Watch and pray, the Lord commandeth, Watch and pray, the Lord commandeth; Watch and

pray, ... 'twill not be long: Soon he'll gath - - -
pray, 'twill not be long, Watch and pray, 'twill not be long: Soon he'll gather home his

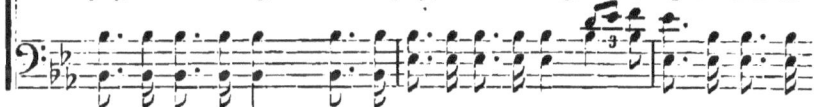

- - - er home his loved ones To the happy vale of song. of song.
loved ones, Soon he'll gather home his loved ones To the happy vale of song. the vale of song.

At the Cross I'll Abide.

I. B.
"And many women were there."—Matt. xxvii. 55.
I. BALTZELL.

1. O   Jesus, Saviour, I long to rest Near the cross where thou hast died;
2. My dy-ing Je-sus, my Saviour God, Who hast borne my guilt and sin,
3. O   Je-sus, Saviour, now make me thine, Never let me stray from thee;
4. The cleansing pow'r of thy blood apply, All my guilt and sin re-move;

For there is hope for the ach-ing breast, At the cross I will   a - bide.
Now wash me, cleanse me with thine own blood, Ever keep me pure and clean,
Oh, wash me, cleanse me, for thou art mine, And thy love is full and free.
Oh, help me, while at thy cross I   lie, Fill my soul with perfect love.

CHORUS.

At the cross   I'll a - bide,   At the cross   I'll a - bide.
At the cross   I'll a-bide,   At the cross   I'll abide;

At the cross I'll abide, There his blood is applied ; At the cross I am sanctified.

Happy in the Love of Jesus.

Henrietta E. Blair.

Wm. J. Kirkpatrick.

1. Bright is the day-star shin-ing for me, Happy in the love of Je - sus;
2. He has redeemed me, I am his own, Happy in the love of Je - sus;
3. How I am honored, how I am blest, Happy in the love of Je - sus:
4. Firm is my anchor, steadfast and sure, Happy in the love of Je - sus;

Now from my bondage grace makes me free, Happy in the love of Je - sus.
Drawn by his mer-cy near to his throne, Happy in the love of Je - sus.
Un - der his ban-ner sweet-ly I rest, Happy in the love of Je - sus.
All things with patience I can endure, Happy in the love of Je - sus.

CHORUS.

Praise from my full heart loudly shall ring, Born of the Spirit, child of a King;

Heir to his glo-ry, now will I sing,—Happy in the love of Je - sus.

The Kingdom Coming.

Mrs. M. B. C. Slade.   R. M. McIntosh. By per.

1. From all the dark pla-ces Of earth's heathen ra-ces, Oh,
2. The sun-light is glanc-ing O'er ar-mies ad-vanc-ing To
3. With shout-ing and sing-ing, And ju-bi-lant ring-ing, Their

see how the thick shadows fly! The voice of sal-va-tion A-
con-quer the king-doms of sin; Our Lord shall pos-sess them, His
arms of re-bell-ion cast down, At last ev-'ry na-tion, The

wakes ev-'ry na-tion, Come o-ver and help us, they cry.
pres-ence shall bless them, His beau-ty shall en-ter them in.
Lord of sal-va-tion Their King and Re-deem-er shall crown!

CHORUS.

The king-dom is com-ing, Oh, tell ye the sto-ry, God's

ban-ner ex-alt-ed shall be! The earth shall be full of his

knowledge and glo - ry, As wa - ters that cov - er the sea!

The Half has Never been Told.

FRANCES R. HAVERGAL.   1 Cor. ii. 9.   R. E. HUDSON. By per.

1. I know I love thee better, Lord, Than an - y earth-ly joy, For
2. I know that thou art nearer still Than an - y earth-ly throng, And
3. Thou hast put gladness in my heart; Then well may I be glad, With -
4. O Saviour, precious Saviour mine! What will thy presence be If

thou hast giv - en me the peace Which noth - ing can de - stroy.
sweet - er is the thought of thee Than an - y love - ly song.
out the se - cret of thy love I could not but be sad.
such a life of joy can crown Our walk on earth with thee?

CHORUS.

The half has never yet been told,   Of love so full and free;
yet been told,

ril.

The half has never yet been told,   The blood—it cleanseth me.
yet been told,   cleanseth me.

A Blessing in Prayer.

E. E. Hewitt.   Wm. J. Kirkpatrick.

1. There is rest, sweet rest, at the Master's feet, There is favor now at the
2. There is grace to help in our time of need, For our friend above is a
3. When our songs are glad with the joy of life, When our hearts are sad with its
4. There is perfect peace though the wild waves roll; There are gifts of love for th

mer - cy seat, For a - ton - ing blood has been sprinkled there; There is
friend in - deed, We may cast on him ev - 'ry grief and care; There is
ills and strife, When the powers of sin would the soul ensnare, There is
seek - ing soul; Till we praise the Lord in his home so fair, There is

REFRAIN.

always a blessing, a blessing in prayer. There's a blessing in prayer, in be -

lieving prayer; When our Saviour's name to the throne we bear, Then a Father'

love will receive us there; There is always a blessing, a blessing in prayer.

Saviour, Blessed Saviour.

Fanny J Crosby.   Jno. R. Sweney.

1. O the joy, the bliss di - vine, Sav - iour, bless - ed Saviour,
2. Once my path was dark as night, Sav - iour, bless - ed Saviour,
3. Thou did'st give thy life for me, Sav - iour, bless - ed Saviour,
4. Make me stronger, day by day, Sav - iour, bless - ed Saviour,

Thus to know and call thee mine, Sav - iour, bless - ed Sav - iour.
Now thy presence makes it bright, Sav - iour, bless - ed Sav - iour.
Now I give my all to thee, Sav - iour, bless - ed Sav - iour.
Still to run the heav'nly way, Sav - iour, bless - ed Sav - iour.

CHORUS.

Not a sor - row, not a care, Thou dost all my burdens bear,

While thy con - stant love I share, Sav - iour, bless - ed Sav - iour.

N

Jesus, My Joy.

Mrs. J. F. Crewdson.　　　　　　　　　　　　　Wm. J. Kirkpatrick.

1. I've found a joy in sor - row, A se - cret balm for pain,
2. I've found a branch for heal - ing Near ev' - ry bit - ter spring,
3. I've found a glad ho - san - na For ev' - ry woe and wail,
4. I've found the Rock of Ag - es, When des - ert wells are dry;

A beau - ti - ful to - mor - row Of sunshine af - ter rain.
A whispered promise steal - ing O'er ev' - ry bro - ken string.
A handful of sweet man - na, When grapes of Es - chol fail.
And af - ter wea - ry stag - es, I've found an E - lim nigh.

CHORUS.

'Tis Jesus, my portion forev - er, 'Tis Jesus, the First and the Last;

A help ver - y present in trou - ble, A shelter from every blast.

5 An Elim with its coolness,
　Its fountains and its shade;
A blessing in its fulness,
　When buds of promise fade.

6 O'er tears of soft contrition
　I've seen a rainbow light;
A glory and fruition,
　So near!—yet out of sight.

Glory, He Saves!

F. A. B.

F. A. BLACKMER.

1. Glo - ry to Je - sus, he saves e - ven me! All my guilt
2. Wand'ring he found me a - far from the fold, Per - ish - ing
3. Safe - ly and sweet - ly he keeps me each day, Gent - ly, so
4. Bless - ed com - pan - ion - ship! cheer - ing 'me so! Sweet - er and

nail - ing to Cal - va - ry's tree; Paid is the debt and my
there in the dark - ness and cold; Half of his good - ness can
gent - ly he leads all the way; An - swers of peace sends he
sweet - er each day shall it grow, Till to be like him I

soul is set free, Glo - ry to Je - sus, he saves!
nev - er be told, Glo - ry to Je - sus, he saves!
down when I pray, Glo - ry to Je - sus, he saves!
joy - ful - ly go, Glo - ry to Je - sus, he · saves!

CHORUS.

Glo - ry, he saves! wondrously saves! Saves a poor sinner like me:

Glo - ry, he saves! wondrously saves! Glory to Je - sus, he saves!

By the Grace of God we'll Meet.

FANNY J. CROSBY.   JNO. R. SWENEY.

1. Thro' the gates of pearl and jasper To the ci-ty paved with gold, When the
2. When the harvest work is ended, And the summer days are past, When the
3. Let us fol-low on with firmness, keeping ev - er in the way Where our

ransomed host shall en - ter, And their gracious Lord be-hold, When they
reap-ers go re-joic - ing To their bright re-ward at last; When the
bles - sed Lord has taught us, To be faith-ful, watch and pray; Then, in

meet in bliss-ful triumph By the tree of life so fair Shall we
white-robed an-gel leads them to the gates of joy so fair, Shall we
garments pure and spotless, By the tree of life so fair, We shall

join the no - ble arm - y, And re - ceive a wel - come there?
join their hap - py num - ber? Will they bid us wel - come there?
sing through endless ag - es With the count - less mil - lions there.

CHORUS.

By the grace . . . . . of God we'll meet . . . . . In the
By the grace of God we'll meet, By the grace of God we'll meet In the

ci - - ty's golden street, Shouting, glo - - - - ry! hal-le-
ci-ty's gold - en street, golden street, Shouting, glo-ry! hal-le-lu-jah! Shouting,

lu - - - jah! At the dear - - - - - Redeem-er's feet.
glo-ry! hal-le-lu-jah! At our dear Re-deem-er's feet, Re-deem-er's feet.

Faithful Guide.

M. M. WELLS. By per.

1. Ho-ly Spir-it, faith-ful guide, Ev-er near the Christian's side;
Gen-tly lead us by the hand, Pil-grims in a des-ert land;
D.C. Whisp'ring soft-ly, wan d'rer, come! Follow me, I'll guide thee home.

D.C.

Wea-ry souls for e'er re-joice, While they hear that sweet-est voice,

2 Ever present, truest Friend,
Ever near thine aid to lend,
Leave us not to doubt and fear,
Groping on in darkness drear,
When the storms are raging sore,
Hearts grow faint, and hopes give o'er,
Whispering softly, wanderer, come!
Follow me, I'll guide thee home.

3 When our days of toil shall cease,
Waiting still for sweet release,
Nothing left but heaven and prayer,
Wond'ring if our names were there;
Wading deep the dismal flood,
Pleading nought but Jesus' blood;
Whispering softly, wanderer, come!
Follow me, I'll guide thee home!

Jesus is Strong to Deliver.

J. P. W.

1. When in the tempest he'll hide us, When in the storm he'll be near;
2. When in my sorrow he found me, Found me, and bade me be whole,
3. Why are you doubting and fearing, Why are you still under sin?
4. You say, "I-am weak, I am helpless, I've tried again and again;" Well,

All the way 'long he will carry us on,—Now we have nothing to fear.
Turn'd all my night into heavenly light, And from me my burden did roll.
Have you not found that his grace doth abound, He's mighty to save, let him in!
this may be true, but it's not what *you* do,'Tis *he* who's the "mighty to save."

CHORUS.

Je-sus is strong to de-liv-er, Mighty to save, mighty to save!

Je-sus is strong to de-liv-er, Je-sus is mighty to save!

From "Highway Songs," by per.

The Morning Draweth Nigh.

FANNY J. CROSBY.　　　　　　　　　　　　　　　　　JNO. R. SWENEY.

1. Oh, ral-ly round the stand-ard Of Christ, our roy-al King; Oh,
2. Tho' long and deep the sha-dows The dreary night may bring, Our
3. To yon-der gold-en reg-ion Our faith now plumes her wing; Our
4. To him who paid our ran-som, And took from death the sting, Be

ral-ly round his stand-ard, And hal-le-lu-jahs sing. For the
lamps are trimm'd and burn-ing, Our hal-le-lu-jahs ring.
hearts with joy are bound-ing, And hal-le-lu-jahs ring.
ev-er-last-ing prais-es, Let hal-le-lu-jahs ring.

CHORUS.

morn - - - ing draweth nigh, For the morn - - -
morning draweth nigh, For the morning draweth nigh, Hal-le-lu-jah! hal-le-

- - - ing draweth nigh; We can see . . . . it in the
lu-jah! yes, the morn-ing draw-eth nigh; We can see it, we can

dis - tance, We shall hear it, we shall hear it by and by. by and by.
see it in the distance,

Softly and Tenderly.

W. L. T.

WILL L. THOMPSON.

Very slow. pp

1. Softly and tenderly Jesus is calling, Calling for you and for me,
2. Why should we tarry when Jesus is pleading, Pleading for you and for me?
3. Time is now fleeting, the moments are passing, Passing from you and from me;
4. Oh! for the wonderful love he has promised, Promised for you and for me;

See on the portals he's waiting and watching, Watching for you and for me.
Why should we linger and heed not his mercies, Mercies for you and for me?
Shadows are gathering, death beds are coming, Coming for you and for me.
Tho' we have sinned he, has mercy and pardon, Pardon for you and for me.

CHORUS.

cres.

Come home, . come home, . Ye who are weary, come home,

pp *ppp* *rit.* *pp*

Earnestly, tenderly Jesus is calling, Calling. O sinner, come home!

Stay Not.

Henrietta E. Blair.   Wm. J. Kirkpatrick.

1. Je - sus is waiting to save you, Bring him your burden of sin;
2. Come when the morning is bright- est, Come in the springtime of youth,
3. Come, and the Saviour will give you Life and its pleasures un - told,
4. Come, for the moments are fly - ing, Come ere they vanish a - way;

Knock at the portals of mer - cy, Jesus will welcome you in.
Come in the vig - or of man - hood, Drink at the fountain of truth.
Come, and his mercy will keep you Guarded and safe in his fold.
Trust not the dawn of to-mor - row, Je - sus is waiting to - day.

CHORUS.

Stay not, stay not, Faith - ful his prom - ise and true;

Stay not, stay not, Now there is par - don for you

202 Praise and Magnify our King.

LIZZIE EDWARDS.   JNO. R. SWENEY.

1. Great is the Lord, who rul - eth o - ver all! Wake, wake and sing,
2. Great is the Lord, who spake and it was done; Wake, wake and sing,
3. Great is the Lord: oh, come with ho - ly mirth; Wake, wake and sing,
4. Great is the Lord, and ho - ly is his name! Wake, wake and sing,

wake, wake and sing; Down at his feet in ad - o - ra - tion fall.
wake, wake and sing; Hon - or and strength, do - min - ion he has won.
wake, wake and sing, Come and re - joice, ye na - tions of the earth.
wake, wake and sing; An - gels and men, his wondrous works proclaim.

CHORUS.

Praise and mag - ni - fy our King. O ye redeemed above, Strike, strike your

harps of love, Hail the Blessed One, Hail the Migh - ty One, Sweet - ly his

wonders tell, Loudly his glory swell, Praise and mag - ni - fy our King.

W. J. K

W. J. KIRKPATRICK.

1. Je - sus, Saviour, great Ex-am- ple, Pat-tern of all pur - i - ty,
2. Lest I wan - der from thy pathway, Or my feet move wea - ri - ly,
3. When temptations fierc- ly low - er, And my shrinking soul would flee,
4. When around me all is darkness, And thy beauties none may see,
5. When death's cold, repulsive finger Leaves its impress on my brow,

I would fol - low in thy footsteps, Dai - ly growing more like thee.
Saviour, take my hand and lead me, Keep me steadfast : more like thee.
Change each weakness in- to pow-er, Keep me spotless : more like thee.
May thy beams, oh, glorious brightness! In effulgence shine through me.
May thy life, with-in me swelling, Keep me sing- ing then as now.

CHORUS.

More like thee, more like thee, Saviour, this my constant pray'r shall be—

More like thee, more like thee,

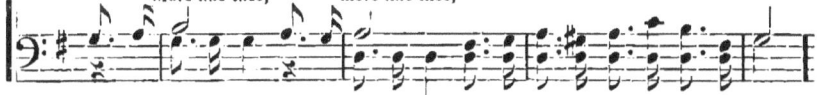

Day by day, where'er I stay, Make me more and more like thee.

Treasures in Heaven.

T. C. O'K.

T. C. O'Kane.

1. There's a crown in heaven for the striving soul, Which the blessed Jesus him-
2. There's a joy in heaven for the mourning soul, Tho' the tears may fall all the
3. There's a home in heaven for the faithful soul, In the many mansions pre-

self will place On the head of each who shall faithful prove, Ev-en
earth-ly night; Yet the clouds of sad-ness will break a-way, And re-
pared a-bove, Where the glo-ri-fied shall for-ev-er sing, Of a

REFRAIN.

unto death, in the heavenly race. Oh, may that crown . . in heaven be
joicing come with the morning light. Oh, may that joy . . . in heaven be
Saviour's free and unbounded love. Oh, may that home . . in heaven be

Oh, may that crown
Oh, may that joy
Oh, may that home

mine. And I a-mong . . the angels shine; Be thou, O
in heaven be mine,

Lord, . . my daily guide, Let me ev-er in thy love a-bide.
Be thou, O Lord, my daily guide,

Showers of Blessing.

"And I will cause the shower to come down in his season."
Ezekiel xxxiv. 26.

JENNIE GARNETT.   JNO. R. SWENEY.

1. Here in thy name we are gathered, Come and revive us, O Lord;
2. O that the showers of bless-ing Now on our souls may descend,
3. There shall be showers of blessing,—Promise that never can fail;
4. Showers of blessing,—we need them, Showers of blessing from thee;

"There shall be showers of bless-ing" Thou hast declared in thy word.
While at the footstool of mer - cy Pleading thy promise we bend!
Thou wilt regard our pe - ti - tion; Sure-ly our faith will pre-vail.
Showers of blessing,—oh, grant them; Thine all the glory shall be.

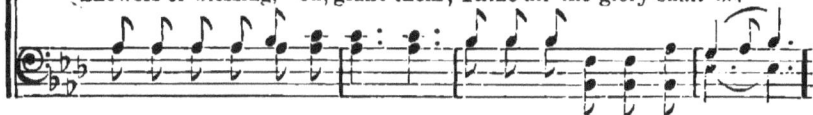

CHORUS.

Oh, gracious-ly hear   us,   Gracious-ly hear us, we   pray:
gracious-ly hear   us,

Pour from thy windows upon   us Showers of blessing to-day.
Lord, pour up-on us

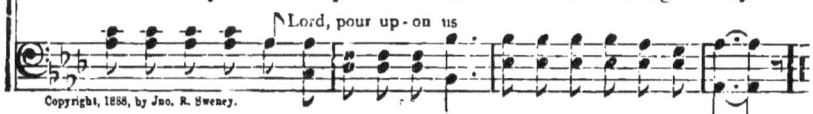

Until Ye Find

Rev. E. H. Stokes, D. D.

Luke xv.

Jno. R. Sweney.

Andante con espress.

1. A - las! a - las! a wayward sheep Had wandered from the fold, Far
2. He sought with many-a footstep sore, From early morn till night; Thro'
3. How long, O Lord, must I still go? How long search for the sheep? They've

o'er the mountains rough and steep, Where howling tempests rolled; The
rock - y wastes, where torrents roar, — All pathways but the right; Then
wandered far a - way, I know, — Discouraged, lo, I weep: How

Shepherd, with a burdened mind, Went forth the missing one to find, The
ied, with sad and burdened mind, The missing I have failed to find, The
long thus go, with burdened mind? "Go," Jesus saith, "until ye find;" The

miss - ing one, far, far a - way, The miss - ing one to find.
miss - ing one, far, far a - way, A - las! I've failed to find.
miss - ing one must not be lost, — Go, seek un - til ye find!

CHORUS.

Go, seek un - til ye find; Go, seek un - til ye find; The

Chorus to last verse :—

Joy! joy! the lost is found; Joy! joy! the lost is found; The

miss-ing one must not be lost,—Go, seek un-til ye find.
miss-ing one, no long-er lost, The miss-ing one is found.

1 I've sought my friends for many-a day,
  Have prayed for many-a year;
Yet, still they wander far away,
  O'er mountains dark and drear;
How long thus seek with burdened mind?
"Seek," Jesus saith, "until ye find;"
  The missing one must not be lost,—
  "Go, seek until ye find!"

5 Lord, at thy word I go again,
  Believing I shall find:
I listened, and a low refrain
  Came to me on the wind;
Led by the sadly joyful sound
I rushed, and, lo, the lost was found!
  Joy! joy! O blessed joy divine!
  The lost one I have found.

Consecration.

Mrs. MARY D. JAMES.   Mrs. JOS. F. KNAPP.

1. My bo-dy, soul, and spirit, Jesus, I give to thee, A con-secrat-ed
2. O Jesus, mighty Saviour, I trust in thy great name, I look for thy sal-
3. Oh, let the fire, descending Just now upon my soul, Consume my humble
4. I'm thine, O blessed Jesus, Wash'd by thy precious blood, Now seal me by thy

REFRAIN.

offering, Thine ev-ermore to be. My all is on the al-tar, I'm
va-tion, Thy promise now I claim.
offering, And cleanse and make me whole.
Spir-it, A sac-rifice to God.

rit.

waiting for the fire; Waiting, waiting, waiting, I'm waiting for the fire.

From "Notes of Joy," by per.

The Firm Foundation.

GEORGE KEITH.

Tune, PORTUGUESE HYMN.

1. How firm a foundation, ye saints of the Lord, Is laid for your
faith in his ex - cel - lent word ! What more can he say, than to
you he hath said, To you, who for re - fuge to Je - sus have
fled ? To you, who for re - fuge to Je - sus have fled ?

2. "Fear not, I am with thee, O be not dismayed, For I am thy
God, I will still give thee aid; I'll strengthen thee, help thee, and
cause thee to stand, Up - held by my gracious, om - ni - po - tent
hand, Up - held by my gracious, om - ni - po - tent hand,

3. "When thro' the deep waters I call thee to go, The riv - ers of
sor - row shall not o - ver- flow; For I will be with thee thy
tri - als to bless, And sanc - ti - fy to thee thy deepest dis -
tress, And sanc - ti - fy to thee thy deep - est dis - tress.

4. "When thro' fie - ry tri - als thy path - way shall lie, My grace all suf -
fi - cient, shall be thy sup - ply, The flame shall not hurt thee; I
on - ly de - sign Thy dross to consume, and thy gold to re -
fine, Thy dross to consume, and thy gold to re - fine.

5 "E'en down to old age all my people shall prove [love;
My sovereign, eternal, unchangeable
And when hoary hairs shall their tem-
ples adorn, [be borne.
Like lambs they shall still in my bosom

6 "The soul that on Jesus still leans for repose.
I will not, I will not desert to his foes;
That soul, though all hell should en-
deavor to shake,
I'll never, no never, no never forsake!"

Let the Blessed Saviour in.

E. E. HEWITT.

WM. J. KIRKPATRICK.

1. Who   stands out-side the   clos-ed door? Rise and let him   in.
2. It   is   the Sav-iour calls to thee, Rise and let him   in.
3. In   pa-tient love he pleading stands, Rise and let him   in.
4. All   night he kept his vig-ils true; Rise and let him   in.

Who   is   it knocking,   o'er and o'er? Rise and let him   in.
He   will come in   and   sup with thee, Rise and let him   in.
The   nail prints still are   in his hands, Rise and let him   in.
Be - hold his locks are   wet with dew; Rise and let him   in.

REFRAIN.

Let him in,   Let him in,   Let the bless-ed Sav-iour
Let him in,   Let him in,

in ;   He is standing at the door, He is knocking o'er and o'er,
Let him in,

Let the blessed Sav-iour   in.

5. O why should he be waiting now?
   Rise and let him in.
   Thy Lord, with glory-circled brow,
   Rise and let him in.

6. Beware, beware ! undo the door;
   Rise and let him in.
   Lest he should leave thee evermore,
   Rise and let him in.

Ah! 'tis the Old, Old Story.

Mrs. C. L. Shacklock.

Wm. J. Kirkpatrick.

1. Ah! 'tis the old, old sto - ry, Tempted and led a - stray,
2. Robbing the heart of lightness, Losing the bloom of youth,
3. But, in an old, old sto - ry, Full of a grace di - vine,

Leaving the path of du - ty, Choosing the e - vil way,
Dimming the eyes' glad brightness, Stilling the voice of truth,
There is a-bun-dant par-don, Ev - en for sin like thine,

Breaking the hearts of mothers, Slighting their fervent prayers,
Missing the pride of man - hood, Missing a no - ble aim,
Now, with a contrite spir - it, Turn from the ways of sin,

Sowing the seed which bringeth On - ly a wealth of tares.
Gaining a ship-wrecked na-ture, Gaining a sul - lied name.
Knock at the gate of heav - en, Entrance thy soul shall win.

CHORUS.

Ah! 'tis the old, old sto - ry, Ah! 'tis the old, old sto - ry,
Last cho.—Yes,'tis the old, old sto - ry, Yes, 'tis the old, old sto - ry,

Ah! 'tis the old, old sto - ry,— Tempted and led a - stray.
Yes, 'tis the old, old sto - ry, Full of a grace di - vine.

Jesus, I come to Thee.

FANNY J. CROSBY.

WM. J KIRKPATRICK.

1. Je - sus, I come to thee, Long-ing for rest; Fold thou thy
2. Je - sus, I come to thee, Hear thou my cry; Save, or I
3. Now let the rolling waves Bend to thy will, Say to the
4. Swift-ly the part-ing clouds Fade from my sight; Yon - der thy

CHORUS.

wea - ry child Safe to thy breast. Rocked on a storm - y sea,
per - ish, Lord, Save or I die.
troubled deep, Peace, peace be still.
bow ap-pears, Love - ly and bright.

Oh, be not far from me, Lord, let me cling to thee, On - ly to thee.

212 Waiting for Me.

FRANK HENDRICKS.　　　　　　　　　　　　　　　JNO. R. SWENEY.

1. I came to the fountain that cleanseth from sin, The life-giving fountain, where
2. He saw me approaching and tender-ly said, To purchase thy ransom my
3. I flew to his mer-cy, O joy-ful surprise, For lo, my Redeem-er had
4. And now in his presence I walk with delight, And feel his protection by

millions have been; I came in my weakness, o'erburdened with care, To
blood I have shed; And if thou art will-ing just now to be-lieve, The
opened mine eyes; I flew to the ref-uge no oth-er could give, And
day and by night; I think of the fountain, so precious and free, Where

find my Redeemer and Saviour was there. Wait - - ing for me, ...
light of my Spirit thy soul shall receive.
faithfully promised for Jesus to live.
Jesus my Saviour was waiting for me.　Waiting for me,　　waiting for me,

wait - - ing for me, . . . Je - - sus my Sav - iour is
waiting for me,　　waiting for me,　Je-sus my Sav-iour is waiting for me,

wait - ing for me; . . . Still . . at the fount . . oft . . . would I
Jesus my Saviour is waiting for me; Still at the fount　oft would I be, Still at the fount

CHORUS.

be .... Where Je - - sus my Sav - iour is wait - ing for me.

oft would I be Where Jesus my Saviour is waiting for me, is waiting, Is waiting for me.

O Rest, Sweet Rest.

MARTHA J. LANKTON.   WM. J. KIRKPATRICK.

1. Thank God for a perfect salvation, That makes me to-day what I am,—
2. He lifts me above the temptations That once could allure me to sin,
3. I live in the constant enjoyment of peace that no language can tell,
4. Praise God for a perfect salvation, My faith is unclouded and bright,

A sanc-ti-fied child of his mercy, Redeemed by the blood of the Lamb.
He saves me from all my transgressions, and cleanseth my spirit within.
Should trials in fu-ture a-wait me, I know with my soul 'twill be well.
My hope like an anchor is steadfast, My mansion of glory in sight.

CHORUS.   *2d time p and rit. ad lib.* Fine.

O rest, sweet rest, I rest in the arms of his love.

O rest, sweet rest,

The Crimson Stream.

Rev. W. J. STEVENSON.   S. B. ELLENBERGER.

1. I stand be-side the crimson stream That flows from Calv'ry's mount,
2. The blood of Christ a-lone will save From guilt, and fear, and care;
3. I claim the promised bles-sing now, Freedom from ev-'ry sin,
4. I sink in-to the crimson stream, Christ's blood is now ap-plied?

And long to wash a-way all sin, With-in its cleans-ing fount.
His blood will sweetly pur-i-fy, When sought in ear-nest prayer.
The power to lead a ho-ly life, With Christ in God shut in.
I rise a-gain, redeemed by him, And whol-ly pur-i-fied.

CHORUS.

Now wash me, now wash me, And cleanse me from sin;
Chorus to last verse:—
Halle-lu-jah! halle-lu-jah! I'm washed from all sin;

Now wash me, now wash me, And I shall be clean.
Halle-lu-jah! halle-lu-jah! Yes, now I am clean.

I'm Saved!

Rev. E. H. Stokes, D D.   Jno. A. Duncan.

1. I'm saved! I'm saved! oh, blessed Lord, I'm sweetly saved in thee;
2. I'm saved! I'm saved! oh, joy sublime! I'm saved from self and sin;
3. Saved at the cross, the blessed cross; Saved without and with - in:
4. I'm saved! I'm saved! I'll tell it here, I'll sing it o'er and o'er;

Saved by thy blood and by thy word, And thine henceforth will be.
I'm saved, I'm saved, oh, bliss di - vine! And love has clos'd me in.
I'm saved, I'm saved, oh, what a loss Who fail this joy to win.
I'm saved in Je - sus, oh, how sweet! I'll sing it ev - er more.

CHORUS.

I'm saved! I'm saved! I'm saved! I'm wash'd in the blood of the Lamb.

I'm saved! I'm saved! I'm saved! I'm wash'd in the blood of the Lamb.

From "Songs of Triumph," by permission.

Blessed be the Name.

W. H. CLARK.

Arranged by WM. J. KIRKPATRICK.

1. All praise to Him who reigns a-bove, In ma - jes - ty su - preme,
2. His name a-bove all names shall stand, Exalt - ed more and more,
3. Re - deem - er, Saviour, Friend of man Once ru - ined by the fall,
4. His name shall be the Counsel - lor, The might- y Prince of Peace,

Who gave his Son for man to die, That he might man re - deem.
At God the Father's own right hand, Where angel hosts a - dore.
Thou hast devised sal - vation's plan, For thou hast died for all.
Of all earth's kingdoms conquer- or, Whose reign shall never cease.

CHORUS.

Blessed be the name, blessed be the name, Blessed be the name of the Lord;

Blessed be the name, blessed be the name, Blessed be the name of the Lord.

5 The ransomed hosts to thee shall bring
  Their praise and homage meet;
  With rapturous awe adore their King,
  And worship at his feet.

6 Then shall we know as we are known,
  And in that world above
  Forever sing around the throne
  His everlasting love.

He has Come.

" Rejoice greatly, O daughter of Zion! Behold, thy King cometh !"

Mrs. J. Knowles.

Jno. R. Sweney.

1. He has come! He has come! My Redeemer has come! He has taken my
2. He has come! He has come! My Love and my Lord! Ev'ry thought of my
3. He has come! He has come! Oh, hap-pi-est heart! He has giv-en his
4. He has come to a-bide: and ho-ly must be The place where my

heart as his own cho-sen home. At last I have giv-en the
be - ing is swayed by his word. He has come, and he reigns in the
word that he will not de-part. What trou-ble can enter; what
Lord deigns to ban-quet with me. And this is my prayer: "Lord,

welcome he sought; He has come, and his coming all gladness has brought.
realm of my soul, And his scep-tre is love! oh, bless-ed con-trol!
e - vil can come To the heart where the God of all peace has his home?
since thou art come, Make meet for thy presence my heart as thy home!"

CHORUS.

He has come! He has come! My Redeemer, my Redeem - er has
He has come! He has come! My Redeem-er, my Redeemer, my Re-

come! His presence is heav'n, My heart is his home! My Redeemer has come!
deemer has come!

218 While the Years are Rolling on.

Harriet B. McKeever.

Jno. R. Sweney.

Recitante.

1.   In   a world so full of weeping, While the years are rolling on, Christian
2.   There's no time to waste in sighing, While the years are rolling on ; Time is
3.   Let us strengthen one anoth - er, While the years are rolling on ; Seek to
4.   Friends we love are quickly flying, While the years are rolling on ; No more

[pursue,
souls the watch are keeping, While the years are rolling on. While our journey we
flying, souls are dying, While the years are rolling on, Loving words a soul may win,
raise a fallen brother, While the years are rolling on. This is work for ev'ry hand
parting, no more dying, While the years are rolling on. In the world beyond the tomb

With the haven still in view, There is work for us to do, While the years are rolling on·
From the wretched paths of sin ; We may bring the wand'rers in, While the years, etc·
Till, Throughout creation's land, Armies for the Lord shall stand, While the years, etc·
Sorrow never more can come, When we meet in that blest home, While the years, etc·

CHORUS

Are   roll - ing   on, are rolling on,   Are   roll- ing   on, are rolling on,

Oh, the joy that we may scatter, While the years are rolling on.

Grace is Free.

EMMA M. JOHNSTON.   WM. J. KIRKPATRICK.

1. There's nothing like the old, old sto - ry, Grace is free, grace is free!
2. There's on - ly hope in trusting Je - sus, Grace is free, grace is free!
3. From age to age the theme is tell-ing, Grace is free, grace is free!

CHO.—There's nothing like, etc.

Fine.

Which saints and martyrs tell in glo - ry, Grace is free, grace is free!
From sin that doomed he died to free us, Grace is free, grace is free!
From shore to shore the strains are swelling, Grace is free, grace is free!

It brought them thro' the flood and flame, By it they fought and overcame,
Who would not tell the sto - ry sweet Of love so wondrous, so complete,
And when that time shall cease to be, And faith is crowned with victo - ry,

Use first four lines as Chorus. D. C.

And now they cry thro' his dear name, Grace is free, grace is free!
And fall in rap - ture at his feet, Grace is free, grace is free!
'Twill sound thro' all e - ter - ni - ty, Grace is free, grace is free!

Abide with Me.

FRANK GOULD.   JNO. R. SWENEY.

1. All the day, ... in sweet commun - ion, . . Je- sus,
2. One by one, ... the ev'ning sha - dows . . Gath-er

1. All the day, in sweet commun- ion, All the day, in sweet communion, Je- sus,
2. One by one the ev'ning sha-dows, One by one the ev'ning shadows, Gath-er

I . . . have walked with thee: . . Do not now . . withdraw thy
dark - - - ly o'er the lea, . . . Yet the light . . of peace re-

I have walked with thee, Jesus, I have walked with thee; Do not now withdraw thy presence, Do not
dark- ly o'er the lea, Gath- er dark-ly o'er the lea, Yet the light of peace remaineth, Yet the

pres - ence, From this hour . . . abide with me. . . . .
main - eth . . If thou still . . . abide with me.

now withdraw thy presence, From this hour abide with me, From this hour abide with me.
light of peace remaineth If thou still abide with me, If thou still abide with me.

CHORUS.

Thou my life, . . . my on - ly guide, . . There is naught in heav'n or
Thou my life,   my on - ly guide,

earth I ask but thee; . . . Hear my prayer, . . . my soul's pe-
I ask but thee;   my soul's pe- ti - tion, Hear my

ti - tion, Go not hence, abide with me.

prayer, my soul's petition, a- bide with me, Go not hence, abide with me.

Oh, to be Like Him.

Mrs. E. C. Ellsworth. Jno. R. Sweney.

DUET.

1. Oh, to be like him, Ten- der and kind, Gen- tle in spir- it,
2. Oh, to be like him, Quick to o - bey, Child-like and truthful,
3. Oh, to be like him, Tempted in vain, Dwell- ing with sinners,

Low- ly in mind; More like to Je - sus, Day af- ter day,
Rea- dy to say, "I and my Fa- ther Purpose have one,
Yet without stain; Giv - ing our life- work Sin- ners to save,

CHORUS.

Filled with his Spirit, Now and al - way. Yes, to be like him,
Thine, not my will, Ev- er be done."
Triumph- ing o - ver Death and the grave.

We must a - bide Near to Our Sa-viour, Close to his side.

222 What a Gath'ring that will be.

J. H. K.　　　"Gather my saints together unto me."—Ps. l. 5.　　J. H. KURZENKNABE.

1. At the sounding of the trumpet, when the saints are gather'd home, We will
2. When the angel of the Lord proclaims that time shall be no more, We shall
3. At the great and final judgement, when the hidden comes to light, When the
4. When the golden harps are sounding, and the angel bands proclaim, In tri-

greet each other by the crystal sea, With the friends and all the lov'd ones there a-
gather, and the saved and ransom'd see, Then to meet again together, on the
Lord in all his glory we shall see; At the bidding of our Saviour, "Come, ye
umphant strains the glorious jubilee; Then to meet and join to sing the song of

crystal sea;

waiting us to come, What a gath'ring of the faithful that will be!
bright ce-lestial shore, What a gath'ring of the faithful that will be!
blessed to my right, What a gath'ring of the faithful that will be!
Moses and the Lamb, What a gath'ring of the faithful that will be!

CHORUS.

What a gath - - - 'ring, gath - - 'ring, At the
What a gath'ring of the loved ones when we'll meet with one an-oth-er,

sounding of the glorious jubi - lee! What a gath - 'ring,
jubilee! What a gath'ring when the friends and all the

From "Song Treasury," by per.

gath - 'ring, What a gath'ring of the faithful that will be!
dear ones meet each other,

By Grace I Will.

E. E. HEWITT.   WM. J. KIRKPATRICK.

1. { Will you go to Je - sus now, dear friend? He is calling you to-day;
   { Will you seek the bright and better land, By "the true and living way?

2. { Would you know the Saviour's boundless love, And his mercy rich and free?
   { Will you seek the saving, cleansing blood, That was shed for you and me.

REFRAIN.

I will, I will! by the grace of God, I will; I will go to Jesus now; I will

heed the gospel call, For the promise is for all; I will go to Je- sus now.

3 Will you consecrate your life to him,
   To be ever his alone?
 And your loving service freely yield,
   To the King upon his throne.

4 Will you follow where the Master
   Choosing only his renown, [leads,
 Will you daily bear the cross for him,
   Till he bids you wear the crown?

Wait, and Murmur Not.

Wm. J. Kirkpatrick.

1. The home where changes never come, Nor pain nor sorrow, toil nor care; Yes!
2. Yet when bow'd down beneath the load By heav'n allow'd, thine earthly lot; Thou
3. If in thy path some thorns are found, O, think who bore them on his brow; If
4. Toil on, nor deem, tho' sore it be, One sigh unheard, one pray'r forgot; The

'tis a bright and blessed home; Who would not fain be resting there?
yearnst to reach that blest a - bode, Wait, meek - ly wait, and murmur not.
grief thy sorrowing heart has found, It reached a ho - li - er than thou.
day of rest will dawn for thee; Wait, meek - ly wait, and murmur not.

CHORUS.

O, wait, meek - ly wait, meek - ly wait, and mur - mur not, O,

wait, meek - ly wait, meekly wait, and murmur not, O, wait, meekly wait,

O, wait, meekly wait, O, wait, and mur - mur not. O, murmur not.

A Shout in the Camp.

FANNY J. CROSBY.　　　　　　　　　　JNO. R. SWENEY.

1. There's a shout in the camp, for the Lord is here, Hal - le - lujah! praise his
2. There's a shout in the camp like the shout of old, Hal - le - lujah! praise his
3. There's a shout in the ranks of the King of kings, Hal - le - lujah! praise his
4. There's a shout in the camp while our souls repeat Hal - le - lujah! praise his

name;　To the feast of his love we again draw near, Praise, oh,
name;　For the cloud of his glo - ry we now be - hold, Praise, oh,
name;　While we drink at the Rock from the living springs, Praise, oh,
name;　There is room for the world at the Saviour's feet, Praise, oh,

praise his name;

CHORUS.

praise his name. Room for the millions! room for all! Halle - lu-jah! praise his

name;　Come to the banquet, great and small, Praise, oh, praise his name.

praise his name;

Is not this the Land of Beulah.

ANON.

ARRANGED.

1. I am dwell-ing on the mountain, Where the gold-en sunlight gleams
2. I can see far down the mountain, Where I wandered wea-ry years,
3. I am drink-ing at the fountain, Where I ev - er would a-bide;

O'er a land whose wondrous beauty Far ex-ceeds my fondest dreams;
Oft - en hin-dered in my jour-ney By the ghosts of doubts and fears,
For I've tast - ed life's pure riv - er, And my soul is sat-is-fied;

Where the air is pure, e - the-real, Laden with the breath of flowers,
Brok-en vows and dis-appointments Thickly sprinkled all the way,
There's no thirst-ing for life's pleasures, Nor a-dorn - ing, rich and gay,

CHO.—Is not this the land of Beu-lah, Blessed, bles - sed land of light,

D. S. Chorus.

They are blooming by the fountain, 'Neath the am - a-ranthine bowers.
But the Spir - it led, un - er-ring, To the land I hold to-day.
For I've found a rich-er treasure, One that fad - eth not a - way.

Where the flow-ers bloom for-ev - er, And the sun is always bright.

4 Tell me not of heavy crosses,
    Nor the burdens hard to bear,
For I've found this great salvation
    Makes each burden light appear;
And I love to follow Jesus,
    Gladly counting all but dross,
Worldly honors all forsaking
    For the glory of the Cross.

5 Oh, the Cross has wondrous glory!
    Oft I've proved this to be true;
When I'm in the way so narrow
    I can see a pathway through;
And how sweetly Jesus whispers:
    Take the Cross, thou need'st not fear
For I've tried this way before thee,
    And the glory lingers near.

Jesus will Save You now.

Henrietta E. Blair. Wm. J. Kirkpatrick.

1. Come, oh, come to the ark of rest,— Je - sus will save you now;
2. Come, oh, come to the ark of grace,— Je - sus will save you now;
3. Come, oh, come to the ark of love,— Je - sus will save you now;
4. Who'll be first to a - rise for prayer? Je - sus will save you now;

Come, with the weight of your guilt oppressed, Je - sus will save you now.
Haste to his arms and his dear embrace, Je - sus will save you now.
Come, like the worn and wea - ry dove, Je - sus will save you now.
Who'll be the first the cross to bear? Je - sus will save you now.

CHORUS.

Come while your cheeks with tears are wet, Come ere the star of life shall set,

Come, and the step you will ne'er re - gret, Je - sus will save you now.

DO RE MI FA SO LA SI

Abiding.

Rev. E. H. Stokes, D.D.   Jno. R. Sweney.

1. My soul for light and love had earnest longings, Oh, how it longed for
2. Oh, how en-riching is this sacred treasure! En-riching to this
3. Oh, yes, I rest, how blessed is the rest-ing! I rest to-day, I'm

fellowship di-vine! I sought it here and there, I sought it ev'rywhere, At
soul, this soul of mine; There's nothing any where Can with this love compare, And
resting all the time; "Come," echoes thro' the air, "Come," and the resting share, And

CHORUS.

last, thro' faith, the holy boon was mine. I'm a - bid - ing, gracious
I henceforth, for-ev- er, Lord, am thine.
Je- sus will be yours as he is mine.

Sav- iour, I'm a - bid- ing in thy precious love to - day; I'm a-

bid - ing, yes, a - bid - ing In thy love, thy precious love, to - day.

Resting at the Cross.

W. J. K.

WM. J. KIRKPATRICK.

1. To the cross of Christ, my Sav-iour, I had brought my weary soul;
2. At the cross, while meekly bow-ing, Je - sus, smiling, bade me live;
3. At the cross, while prostrate ly - ing, Je- sus' blood flowed o'er my soul,
4. At the cross I'm calmly rest - ing, Ev - 'ry moment now is sweet;

Burdened, faint, and broken-heart - ed, Praying, "Je- sus, make me whole."
"I have died for your transgressions, And I free - ly all for - give."
All my guilt and sin were cov - ered, And he whispered, "Child, be whole."
I am tast-ing of his glo - ry, I am rest-ing at his feet.

CHORUS.

Glo - ry, glo - ry be to Je - sus, I am counting all but dross,

I have found a full sal - va - tion, I am resting at the cross;

I'm resting (at the cross), I'm resting (at the cross), I'm resting at the cross.

DO RE MI FA SO LA SI

Rejoicing Evermore.

JOHN NEWTON.   R. E. HUDSON.

1. Tho' troubles as-sail, and dang-ers affright, Tho' friends should all!
2. The birds, without barn or storehouse, are fed; From them let us
3. When Sa-tan appears to stop up our path, And fills us with
4. He tells us we're weak,—our hope is in vain: The good that we

CHORUS.—Yes, I will re-joice, re-joice in the Lord, Yes, I will re-

fail, and foes all u-nite, Yet one thing secures us, whatev - er be-
learn to trust for our bread, His saints, what is fitting, shall ne'er be de-
fears, we tri-umph by faith; He cannot take from us, tho' oft he has
seek we ne'er shall obtain: But when such suggestions our graces have

joice, re-joice in the Lord, Yes, I will re-joice, re-joice in the

D. C.

tide, The prom-ise as-sures us,— the Lord will pro - vide.
nied, So long as 'tis written,— the Lord will pro - vide.
tried, The heart-cheer-ing promise,— the Lord will pro - vide.
tried, This ans-wers all questions,— the Lord will pro - vide.

Lord, Will joy in the God of my sal - va - tion.

5 No strength of our own, nor goodness
    we claim;   [name:
Our trust is all thrown on Jesus' great
In this our strong tower for safety we
    hide;
The Lord is our power,—the Lord will
    provide,

6 When life sinks apace, and death is in
    view,
The word of his grace shall comfort us
    through: [our side,
Not fearing or doubting, with Christ on
We hope to die shouting,—the Lord will
    provide.

From "Salvation Echoes," by per.
Pub. at Alliance, O.

DO RE MI FA SO LA SI

FANNY J. CROSBY.

JNO. R. SWENEY.

1. Tho' my sins were once like crimson red, To the healing stream my feet were led,
2. At the door of faith I entered in, And to him confessed my guilt and sin,
3 Tho' my heart was all I had to give, Yet he smiled and bade me look and live,
4. I will sing his pow'r from death to save, I will sing his triumph o'er the grave,

In the precious blood my Sav-iour shed He washed me white as snow.
With his own dear hand he washed me clean, He washed me white as snow.
What a calm sweet peace did I receive,—He washed me white as snow.
I will sing, while crossing Jordan's wave, He washed me white as snow.

CHORUS.

O, my joy - ful song henceforth shall be, 'Tis the blood of Je - sus

cleans-eth me, Cleans-eth, cleans-eth, Oh, yes, it cleanseth me.

Behold the Bridegroom.

"And at midnight there was a cry made, Behold, the bridegroom cometh : go ye out to meet him."—Matt. xxv. 6.

R. E. H.   R. E. Hudson.

1. Are you ready for the Bridegroom When he comes, when he comes? Are you
2. Have your lamps trimm'd and burning When he comes, when he comes; Have your
3.   We will all go out to meet him When he comes, when he comes; We will
4.   We will chant al - le - lu-ias When he comes, when he comes; We will

ready for the Bridegroom When he comes, when he comes, Behold! he cometh!
lamps trimm'd and burning When he comes, when he comes, He quickly cometh!
all go out to meet him When he comes, when he comes; He surely cometh!
chant   al - le - lu-ias When he comes, when he comes: Lo! now he cometh!

D.S.—Behold! he cometh!

Fine.

*be-hold! he cometh! Be robed and read - y, for the Bridegroom comes.
he quick-ly cometh, O soul, be read - y when the Bridegroom comes.
he sure - ly cometh! We'll go to meet him when the Bridegroom comes.
lo! now he cometh! Sing al - le - lu - ia! for the Bridegroom comes.

be - hold! he cometh! Be robed and read - y, for the Bridegroom comes.

CHORUS.   D.S.

Behold the Bridegroom, for he comes, for he comes!
Behold the Bridegroom, for he comes, for he comes

DO RE MI FA SO LA SI

Sallie Smith.

Jno. R. Sweney.

1. I have found a friend di - vine, Wont you love him too?
2. Oh, how dear his name to me, Wont you love him too?
3. Heav - y - lad - en, care - oppressed, Wont you love him too?
4. Cast your bur - den at his feet, Wont you love him too?

I am his and he is mine, Wont you love him too?
None can save your soul but he, Wont you love him too?
How he longs to give you rest, Wont you love him too?
There is par - don pure and sweet, Wont you love him too?

CHORUS.

Wont you love my Je - sus, My pre-cious, precious Je - sus?

Wont you love my Je - sus? He is waiting now for you.

Oh! 'tis Wonderful.

E. A. Barnes.   Jno R. Sweney.

Moderato.

1. In the gospel's sweet old sto - ry, Lo! I read its gold - en theme,
2. Sin its se - cret work was ply - ing, Adding guilt with ev - 'ry day,
3. To his love I was a strang - er, To his call I gave no heed,

How the Prince of life and glo - ry came to suf - fer and re - deem.
Till I read that Christ in dy - ing, Died to take my guilt a - way.
Till at last I saw my dan - ger, Found the Friend I stood in need.

REFRAIN.

Oh! 'tis wonderful, won - der - ful, Yes, 'tis wonderful, won - der - ful!

Oh! 'tis wonder - ful, won - der - ful, The sto - ry of his love.

By permission.

Open the Door.

Henrietta E. Blair.　　　　　　　　　　　　　　　　　　　W. J. K.

1. Je - sus, the Saviour, is waiting and knocking, Standing to-day at the
2. Long he has called thee and thou hast refused him, Long he has waited thy
3. What if the lamp of thy life should be darken'd? What if the Saviour should
4. While he is calling and waits to be gracious Haste to admit him, the

door of thy heart; Say, wilt thou o - pen and glad - ly receive him,
ans - wer to hear; Still he is knocking; how canst thou be silent?
call thee no more? Think of the anguish, thy spir - it ap - palling,
warn - ing o - bey; While he is holding the scep - tre of pardon,

CHORUS.

Or wilt thou bid him in sor - row de-part? O - pen the door, 'tis the
Now at this moment thy doom may be near.
Knowing the day of pro - ba - tion is o'er.
Quickly receive him—no long - er de - lay.

Saviour knocking, Patiently knocking to-day at thy heart; O - pen the

ad lib.

door, 'tis the Saviour knocking, Knocking, knocking,—must he depart?

I am glad.

Lizzie Edwards.   Jno. R. Sweney.

Andante.

1. I will tell the world around me How my blessed Saviour found me, How he
2. From the cold and barren mountain To the precious, cleansing fountain How he
3. In his mer-cy I am hiding, In his shadow still a-biding: He is

broke the chains that bound me, And my sins he washed away;   Oh, my
led me like a shepherd, When my soul was far a-way;   To the
teach-ing me with patience, How to la-bor, watch, and pray. I am

grateful heart is glowing, And with joy is overflowing; I will praise my dear Re-
cross I now am clinging, And my happy song is ringing; I will praise my dear Re-
trusting and believing, I am asking and receiving; I will praise my dear Re-

CHORUS.

deem-er, I will praise him all the day. I am glad, I am glad, I am

glad that Je-sus found me! With his precious blood he bought me: Halle-lu - jah to his name! I enjoy a perfect blessing, And his constant love pos-

sess- ing, Ev - 'ry promise he has left me For my-self I now can claim.

Away to Jesus.

FANNY L. JOHNSON.   J. R. S.

1. A lit - tle while to sow and reap, And then a-way to Je - sus; A
2. A lit - tle while on earth to meet, And then a-way to Je - sus; To
3. A lit - tle while our crown to win, And then a-way to Je - sus; A
4. A lit - tle while to part in tears, And then a-way to Je - sus; A

Fine.

lit - tle while our watch to keep, And then a-way to Je - sus.
feel the bliss of un-ion sweet, And then a-way to Je - sus.
few more vic-t'ries o - ver sin, And then a-way to Je - sus.
few more days, a few more years, And then a-way to Je - sus.

D. S. — feast the soul, while ag - es roll, And shout the love of Je - sus.

CHORUS.   D.S.

To Je - sus, to Je - sus, A - way, a - way to Je - sus, To

Give me Jesus.

FANNY J. CROSBY.
JNO R. SWENEY.

1 Take the world, but give me Je - sus,—All its joys are but a name;
2. Take the world, but give me Je - sus, Sweetest com - fort of my soul;
3. Take the world, but give me Je - sus, Let me view his constant smile ;
4. Take the world, but give me Je - sus, In his cross my trust shall be,

But his love a - bid - eth ev - er, Thro' e - ter - nal years the same.
With my Sav - iour watching o'er me I can sing, though billows roll.
Then throughout my pilgrim jour - ney Light will cheer me all the while.
Till, with clear - er, brighter vis - ion, Face to face my Lord I see.

CHORUS.

Oh, the height and depth of mer - cy! Oh, the length and breadth of love!

Oh, the ful - ness of redemption, Pledge of end - less life a - bove!

My Spirit is Free.

W. A. S.

Rev. W. A. Spencer, D. D.

1. I fol-low the footsteps of Je-sus, my Lord, His Spir-it doth
2. A lep-er he found me, pol-lu-ted by sin, From which he a-
3. A cap-tive in woe to my pris-on of night, The Mas-ter hath
4. Proclaim it, 'tis done, full sal-va-tion is wrought For sin-ners from

lead me a - long; I walk in the pathway made plain by his word,
lone can set free; He spake, in his mer-cy, "I will, be thou clean,"
o-pen'd the door; Shout a-loud of deliv'rance, ye an-gels of light,
sor-row and woe; Sing a-loud of his grace who my pardon has bought,

REFRAIN.

And he fills all my soul with this song. Glo-ry to God, my
And he in-stant-ly pur-i-fied me.
Praise his name, O my soul, ev - er - more.
For his blood washes whit-er than snow.

spir - it is free, Glo-ry to God, he pur-i-fies me; I'm

walking the thorn-path, but joyful I'll be While following Jesus, my Lord.

By permission.

Wonderful Love of Jesus.

"The love of Christ, which passeth knowledge."
Eph iii. 19.

E. D. Mund.   E. S. Lorenz.

1. In vain in high and ho-ly lays My soul her grateful voice would raise; For
2. A joy by day, a peace by night, In storms a calm, in darkness light; In
3. My hope for pardon when I call, My trust for lift-ing when I fall; In

who can sing the worthy praise Of the won-derful love of Je - sus?
pain a balm, in weakness might, Is the won-derful love of Je - sus.
life, in death, my all in all, Is the won-derful love of Je - sus.

CHORUS.

Won-derful love! won-derful love! Won-der-ful love of Je - sus!

Wonder-ful love! won-derful love! Wonder-ful love of Je - sus!

From "Holy Voices," by per.

Safe in the Glory Land.

JAMES L. BLACK.　　　　　　　　　　　　　　　JNO. R. SWENEY.

1. In the good old way where the saints have gone, And the
2. In the good old way like the ransomed throng, Un - to
3. In the good old way with a stead - fast faith, In the
4. Tho' our feet must stand on the cold, cold brink Of the

King leads on be - fore us, We are travelling home to the
Zi - on now re - turn - ing, We are travelling home at the
bonds of love and un - ion, What a joy is ours for the
Jor - dan's storm - y riv - er, With the King we'll cross to the

CHORUS.

heavenly hills, With the day-star shining o'er us. Travelling home to the
King's command, And our lamps are trimm'd and burning.
King we see, And with him we hold communion.
oth - er side, And we'll sing his praise for-ev - er.

man - sions fair, Crowns of re - joic - ing and life to wear;

O what a shout when we all get there, Safe in the glo - ry land!

Q

Always Abounding.

"Always abounding in the work of the Lord."—1 Cor. xv. 58.

E. A. BARNES.   WM. J. KIRKPATRICK.

1. Be earnest, my brothers, in word and in deed, Be active in reaping and
2. Be ready, my brothers, his call to o-bey, In seeking the erring and
3. Be zealous, my brothers, the light to extend, And unto all nations the

sow-ing the seed; And thus in the vineyard, with Je-sus to lead, Be
show-ing the way; And thus as his servants, remem-ber, we pray, Be
gos-pel to send; And thus, till the harvest in glo-ry shall end, Be

REFRAIN.

always abounding in the work of the Lord. Be always abounding in the

work of the Lord, Be always abounding in the work of the Lord; Be earnest, be

active, re-lying on his word, Be always abounding in the work of the Lord.

Lord, I Come Repenting.

Rev. Arthur T. Pierson, D. D.

Jno. R. Sweney.

1. Lord, I come re - pent - ing; Self and sin I long have sought,
2. Lord, I come be - liev - ing; Ev - 'ry prom - ise hum - bly claim,
3. Lord, I come o - bey - ing; Lo, I come to do thy will,

Wick - ed works my life has wrought, Sins of speech and secret thought,
Trust the one and on - ly Name, Yes - ter-day, to - day the same,
And, through seeming good or ill, Fol - low in thy footsteps still:

CHORUS.

Now I come re-pent - ing. Bowing low before thy throne, Trusting in thy
Now I come be - liev - ing.
Now I come o - bey - ing.

blood a - lone, Own me, Saviour, as thine own, While I come { repenting.
{ believing.
{ obeying.

Coming Victory.

G. W. Collins.   Wm. J. Kirkpatrick.

1. There's a murmur in the valley, and there's music on the hills, There's a
2. Lo! it whispers of the coming of a bet-ter, brighter day, And it
3. Hear this army's heav-y footfall, how it shakes the solid ground, As it
4. Soon will come a day of gladness, when the victo-ry we gain, And our

message full of promise ev-'rywhere; We can read it in the sunbeams as they
bids us watch to see the glorious dawn; When the mists of sin and sorrow shall be
gathers to do battle for the right; Hear the ringing voice of captains, and the
land, redeemed and ransomed, shall be free; We will join the voice of millions as they

dance up-on the rills, We can catch the floating cadence in the air.
driv-en far a-way, As the arm-y in its triumph marches on.
thrilling bu-gle sound, They are calling us to muster for the fight.
shout the glad refrain To the welcome song of Freedom's Jubi-lee.

CHORUS.

On-ward, onward now the arm-y still advanc-es. See its ban-ners

wav-ing in the sun;   On-ward,   on-ward now, let
                    yes, wav-ing:

vic-t'ry be the watchword, The battle by the bal-lot must be won!

I'll be There.

ISAAAC WATTS.

Adapted by WM. J. KIRKPATRICK.

1. { There is a land of pure delight, Where saints immor-tal reign;
In - fi - nite day ex-cludes the night, And pleasures ban-ish pain. }

2. { There ev - er-last-ing spring abides, And nev - er-with'ring flowers;
Death, like a narrow sea, divides This heavenly land from ours. }

REFRAIN.

I'll be there, I'll be there, When the first trumpet sounds I'll be there,
I'll be there,

I'll be there, I'll be there, When the first trumpet sounds I'll be there.

3 Sweet fields beyond the swelling flood
Stand dressed in living green;
So to the Jews old Canaan stood,
While Jordan rolled between.

4 Could we but climb where Moses stood,
And view the landscape o'er, [flood
Not Jordan's stream, nor death's cold
Should fright us from the shore.

Pray for the Fallen.

MARTHA J. LANKTON.   WM. J. KIRKPATRICK.

1. Pray for the fal-len! oh, think of them kindly, Take them to Jesus, his
2. Pray for the fal-len! oh, do not forsake them, Slaves to the tempter who
3. Pray for the fal-len, the world has renounced them! Keen are its glances, its
4. Pray for the erring! oh, think of them kindly They are our neighbors, tho'

mercy implore; Tho' they have wander'd, and sad their condition, Prayer and our
laughs at their pain; Fast in the fet-ters he forged to deceive them, Pi-ty and
censure is cold; Yet the dear Saviour will gently receive them, He will not
far they have stray'd; They are our brothers: go forth to their rescue! Give them our

CHORUS.

efforts their souls may restore. Pray for them earnestly, pray for them faithfully,
help them again and a-gain.
turn them away from his fold.
friendship, our comfort, our aid. Pray   earnest-ly, pray   faith-ful-ly,

Prayers will be answered thro' Je-sus' dear name; Pray for them fervent-ly,
Pray   fer-vent-ly,

lov-ing, and tenderly,—Prayer and our ef-forts the lost may reclaim.

The Rum Saloon shall Go.

Rev. John O. Foster. A. M.　　　　　　　　　Jno. R. Sweney.

1. A wave is roll-ing o'er the land, With heavy un-der-tow;
2. Its doom is writ-ten on the sky, A-bove the shining bow;
3. We've stood the wretched, bit-ter moans Full long enough, you know;
4. The land is tired of the curse, The people have said so;

And voic-es sounding on the strand; The rum sa-loon shall go.
For in-dig-na-tion now is high, The rum sa-loon shall go.
And soon we'll speak in thunder tones, Un-less they close and go.
And if it halts we'll make it worse, And help them soon to go.

CHORUS.

Shall go,　we know,　Shall go,　we
Shall go,　　we know,　Shall go,

know; A cry is sounding o'er the land, The rum saloon shall go.
we know;

Is there Any One Here.

Martha J. Lankton.   Wm. J. Kirkpatrick.

1. Is there an-y one here that is will-ing to-day On Je-sus the
2. Is there an-y one here that is try-ing to-day The fet-ters of
3. Is there an-y one here that is wea-ry to-day, Or la-den, or
4. Hear the Saviour's sweet voice while he calls thee again, O come, and be-

Lord to be-lieve? Is there an-y poor soul that is longing to-day The
e-vil to break? An-y read-y to fol-low the Saviour to-day, And
sor-row oppressed? Is there any sad heart that is praying to-day To
lieve and o-bey; He is waiting to bless, he will comfort thee now! He

CHORUS.

gift of his grace to re-ceive.   Come   un-to me,
take up the cross for his sake.
find in the Sav-iour a rest?   Come un-to me,   come un-to me,
nev-er turned an-y a-way.

Come   un-to me;   Je-sus is call-ing,
Come un-to me,   come un-to me;

ad lib.

call-ing now to thee, Come, oh, come un-to me. un-to me.

Leading Souls to Jesus.

J. E. Rankin, D. D.

Jno. R. Sweney.

1. Leading souls to Jesus who are sad and lost, Who upon life's waters have been
2. Leading souls to Jesus, telling them the way Out of nature's darkness into
3. Leading souls to Jesus from their want and sin, Setting up his kingdom with its
4. Leading souls to Jesus, as the stars to shine, In some humbly station, Master,

tempest-tossed; All the heavy-laden, burdened with their load, Whisp'ring of sal-
God's own day; Kneeling with the sinner at the Saviour's feet, Even angels
peace within; 'Till the Spirit witness in them o'er and o'er, Cleans'd are thy trans-
be it mine; With forgiven sin-ners, not alone, to stand When I rise to

CHORUS.

vation thro' the Lamb of God. Leading souls to Jesus! oh, may this be mine,
can not know of work more sweet.
gressions: go, and sin no more.
glo-ry in the bet-ter land.

Till I cross the riv - er to that home divine; Sowing by all wa - ters,

till the great day come, When with joy the reapers shout the harvest home.

The Universal Call.

Arthur T. Pierson, D. D.

Jno. R. Sweney.

1. The Spir - it and the Bride say, "Come! And drink of the water of
2. "O, Come!" Let ev - 'ry one who hears To all who are near him now
3. Who - ev - er will, come, taste and see! Your longings the Saviour can

1. The Spirit and the Bride say, "Come!" The Spirit and the Bride say, "Come! And drink of the water, and
2. "O, Come!" Let ev'ry one who hears, "O, Come!" Let ev'ry one who hears, To all who are near him, to
3. Whoever will, come, taste and see! Whoever will, come, taste and see! Your longings the Saviour, your

life." . . . . O, bles - sed call, Good news for all, Who
say, ... "I heard the sound, The stream I found, Be-
fill! . . . . The stream is free To you and me, And

drink of the water of life." O, blessed call, Good news to all, O, blessed call, Good news to all, Who
all who are near him now say, I heard the sound, The stream I found, I heard the sound, The stream I found, Be-
longings the Saviour can fill! The stream is free To you and me, The stream is free To you and me, And

CHORUS.

tire of sin and strife. . . . The Spirit says, Come, The Bride says, Come, And
hold the living way!" . .
who - soev - er will! . . .

tire of sin and strife. Who tire of sin and strife. The Spirit says come, come, The Bride says come, come, And
hold the living way!" Behold the living way!"
whosoever will! And whosoever will!

drink of the wa - ter of life; . . . . The Spir - it says,

drink of the water, and drink of the water of life, the water of life; The Spirit says, come,

Come, The Bride says, Come, And drink of the water of life. . . . . .
come, The Bride says, come, come, And drink of the water of life, And drink of the water of life.

Each Heart Thy Temple.

LAURA MILLER. JNO. R. SWENEY.

1. Thou chief among ten thousand, More love-ly far than all,
2. We come, as thou hast taught us, Thy mer-its, Lord, we plead,
3. We know that thou art with us, We feel thy power di-vine;
4. Our souls, and all with-in us, We con-se-crate to thee,

Fine.

Re-veal thyself in glo-ry, While on thy name we call.
Be-cause thou liv-est ev-er, For us to in-ter-cede.
Thy Spir-it bear-eth wit-ness That we through grace are thine.
And pray that in our weak-ness Thine arm our strength may be.

D. S.—Now make each heart thy tem-ple, And there henceforth a-bide.

CHORUS. D. S.

Thou chief a-mong ten thousand, Our on-ly faith-ful Guide,

Copyright, 1886, by John J. Hood.

Companionship with Jesus.

Mary D. James.　　　　　　　　　　　　　Wm. J. Kirkpatrick.

1. Oh, bless-ed fel-low-ship divine! Oh, joy supremely sweet! Com-
2. I'm walking close to Je-sus' side, So close that I can hear The
3. I'm lean-ing on his lov-ing breast, Along life's weary way; My
4. I know his shelt'ring wings of love Are always o'er me spread, And

pan-ion-ship with Je-sus here Makes life with bliss re-plete. In
soft-est wisp-ers of his love, In fel-low-ship so dear, And
path, il-lumined by his smiles, Grows brighter day by day. No
tho' the storms may fiercely rage, All calm and free from dread, My

un-ion with the pur-est one I find my heav'n on earth be-gun.
feel his great, al-might-y hand Protects me in this hos-tile land.
foes, no woes my heart can fear, With my al-might-y Friend so near.
peace-ful spir-it ev-er sings, "I'll trust the cov-ert of thy wings."

CHORUS.

Oh, wondrous bliss! oh, joy sublime! I've Je-sus with me all the time.

Oh, wondrous bliss! oh, joy sublime! I've Je-sus with me all the time.

At the Cross.

R. Kelso Carter.   Arr. by E. E. Nickerson.

1. O Je-sus, Lord, thy dy-ing love Hath pierced my con-trite heart;
2. A-mid the night of sin and death Thy light hath filled my soul;
3. I kiss thy feet, I clasp thy hand, I touch thy bleed-ing side;
4. My Lord, my light, my strength, my all, I count my gain but loss;

Now take my life, and let me prove How dear to me thou art.
To me thy lov-ing voice now saith, Thy faith hath made thee whole.
O let me here for-ev-er stand, Where thou wast cru ci - fied.
For-ev-er let thy love enthrall, And keep me at the cross.

CHORUS.

At the cross, at the cross, where I first saw the light, And the

bur-den of my heart roll'd a - way, It was there by

faith I receiv'd my sight, And now I am hap-py night and day!

254. All for Me, All for Thee.

Rev. Alfred J. Hough.　　　　　　　　　　　　　　　　Jno R. Sweney

1. Saviour, I have heard thee pleading, Passionate-ly in-ter-ceding,
2. Thou didst stoop in thy compassion To be found in human fashion,
3. Moved by love di-vine and tender, Thou didst joyful - ly sur-ren-der

Seen thy great heart broken, bleeding, All for me, all for me;
And en-dure thy nameless pas-sion All for me, all for me;
Pal - ac - es of rest and splendor All for me, all for me;

Lo, I come, the past la-menting, For the wast-ed years repent-ing,
In thy name I come be-liev-ing, Of thy grace with joy re-ceiving,
Now my soul to life a-wak-ing Finds her highest joy in breaking

And my life henceforth pre-sent-ing All for thee, all for thee.
And the world be-hind me leav-ing, All for thee, all for thee.
Bonds that bound her, and for-sak-ing All for thee, all for thee.

4 'Neath the cross I see thee bending,
To the place of skulls ascending,
None attending, none befriending,
　All for me, all for me;
Now my heart with thy life beating
To each cross shall give glad greeting,
While my lips are still repeating
　All for thee, all for thee.

5 In thy Father's glory sharing,
And the crown of ages wearing,
Thou art now a home preparing
　All for me, all for me;
With the souls of thy befriending,
Saved from sorrow never-ending,
Shall my song be heard ascending
　All for thee, all for thee.

Marching On.

JENNIE GARNETT.

WM. J. KIRKPATRICK.

1. With our col-ors waving bright in the blaze of gos-pel light We are
2. Oft the tempter we shall meet, but we will not fear de-feat, Though his
3. We have gird-ed on the sword and the ar-mor of the Lord, We have
4. Soon we'll reach the pearly gate, where the blessed army wait, Soon their

marshall'd on the world's great field; great field; We are ready for the strife and the
arrows at our ranks may fly; may fly; Thro'a Saviour's mighty love more than
ta-ken up the cross he bore; he bore; Oh, the trophies we shall win, oh, the
welcome, welcome song may ring; may ring; When we lay our armor down and re-

bat-tle work of life, Ev - er trusting in the Lord our shield.
conquerors we shall prove, Shouting, Glo-ry be to God on high.
vic-tory o - ver sin, When the bat-tle and the strife are o'er!
ceive a star-ry crown, Shouting, Glo-ry be to God our King.

CHORUS.

Glo-ry to God! we are marching, marching on, Marching to a home above;

Glo-ry to God! we are marching, marching on, Happy in a Saviour's love.

The Open Arms.

Henrietta E. Blair.

Wm. J. Kirkpatrick.

1. Oh, why are you slighting the Saviour, So patient, for-giv-ing, and true?
2. Once led as a lamb to the slaughter, He suffered, and languished, and died ;
3. A - gain the dear Saviour is call-ing, O turn ye, for why will ye die?
4. A - gain the dear Saviour is pleading, Oh, look to his mer-cy and live ;

The arms of his mer-cy are o-pen; He of-fers a welcome to you.
And now, in his ten-der compas-sion, He shows you his hands and his side.
Your sun may go down in a moment, The ar-row of death may be nigh.
The pleasures of time are but fleet-ing. Then trust not the promise they give.

CHORUS.

O come to the arms that are wait - ing, They long have been
Come, come, come to the arms that are waiting, waiting, Come, they long have been

wait-ing for you; Oh, come . . . to your lov-ing Re-
wait-ing for you, waiting for you ; Come, come, come to your lov-ing Re-

poco rit.

deem - - er, So gen - tle, forgiving, and true.
deemer, your loving Redeemer, Gentle, gentle, forgiving, and true, forgiving and true.

Blessed are the Pure in Heart.

L. L. P.　　　　　　　　Matt. v. 8.　　　　　　　L. L. PICKETT.

1. Blessed are the pure in heart, Soul and bod - y ho - ly, clean,
2. Such shall see our God, we read, We believe this precious word;
3. Yes, we'll see him as he is, When this mor - tal vail is rent,
4. Faith e'en sees him in this life, Walking in his glorious light;

Washed throughout in eve - ry part, Saved and cleansed from every sin.
He'll supply our eve - ry need, 'Tis the promise of our Lord.
In the heavenly land of bliss, When our earth - ly life is spent.
'Midst earth's trouble, toil and strife, He is with us day and night.

CHORUS.

Blessed are the pure in heart, They shall see our heavenly King,

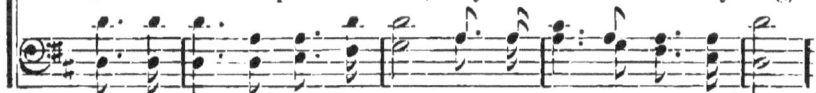

Nev - er from his side de - part, Safe - ly rest beneath his wing.

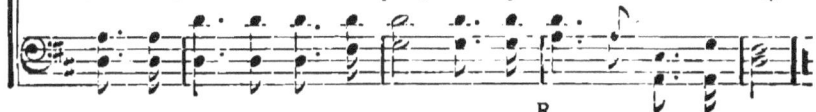

R

Standing on the Promises.

R. K. C.

R. Kelso Carter.

1. Standing on the prom-is - es of Christ my King, Thro' e - ter - nal
2. Standing on the prom-is - es that can - not - fail, When the howling
3. Standing on the prom-is - es I now can see Per - fect, present
4. Standing on the prom-is - es of Christ the Lord, Bound to him e -
5. Standing on the prom-is - es I can - not fall, Listening ev - ery

a - ges let his prais-es ring; Glo - ry in the highest, I will shout and sing,
storms of doubt and fear as-sail, By the liv - ing Word of God I shall pre - vail,
cleansing in the blood for me; Standing in the liberty where Christ makes free,
ter - nally by love's strong cord, O - vercoming dai - ly with the Spir-its' sword,
moment to the Spir-its' call, Rest-ing in my Saviour, as my all in all,

CHORUS.

Standing on the promises of God. Stand - ing, stand - ing,

Standing on the promises, Standing on the promises,

Standing on the promis-es of God my Saviour; Stand - - ing,

Standing on the promis- es,

stand - - ing, I'm standing on the promis- es of God.

Standing on the prom- is- es,

From "Songs of Perfect Love," by per.

Henrietta E. Blair.   Wm. J. Kirkpatrick.

1. Poor, starving soul, there's room for thee Within thy Fa-ther's home;
2. Thy Father waits; what keeps thee back? Behold his pleading face!
3. O, lin-ger not, the time is short, Its sands are ebb-ing fast;

Why linger still? there's bread to spare; Come in,—no longer roam,—
His circling arms would clasp thee now; O, seek his dear em-brace;
This hour is thine,—improve it well,—This hour,—perhaps thy last;

Come in,—be-hold, thy Fa-ther calls; His love for thee is great;
He longs to hear thee say, for-give; He mourns thy hap-less state;
Come in, while yet thy Father pleads, Slight not his love so great;

Fine.

Come in, come in,—he bids thee come; Why stand outside the gate?

D. S.—Come in, come in, there's room for thee; Why stand outside the gate?

CHORUS.   *D. S.*

Out-side the gate, out-side the gate, O soul, no long-er wait;

Let Me in the Life=boat.

L. H. EDMUNDS.

Arr. by WM. J. KIRKPATRICK.

1. Cheer up, wea-ry sail-or; your ship is a-drift, You've lost all your
2. The seas, dark and heav-y, sweep o-ver the deck, Your ef-forts no
3. The good gos-pel life-boat, e-ter-nal-ly planned, Was built by the
4. And now, Christian sail-or, you're tru-ly a-float, And heart-i-ly
5. O, hap-py the course that no billows can thwart, And whether the

bearings; your eyes upward lift, The shadows are break-ing, and
long-er de-struc-tion can check, Your ves-sel is sink-ing, a-
Sa-viour and launched by his hand, Such won-der-ful love we can
sing-ing sal-va-tion's glad note, Reach out hands of mer-cy, help
voy-age shall be lengthy or short, Our Cap-tain will bring us to

light thro' the rift Shows Je-sus, swiftly coming with the life-boat.
ban-don the wreck! Let Je-sus take and save you in the life-boat.
ne'er un-derstand, The love that seeks and saves us in the life-boat.
souls to the boat, And keep on getting oth-ers in the life-boat.
heaven's bright port; All praise to him who saved us in the life-boat.

CHORUS.

Let me in the life-boat! let me in the life-boat! See the storm it grandly braves,

Let me in the life-boat! let me in the life-boat! Jesus bear me safely o'er the waves.

6 Our friends over yonder, on Glory's bright shore,
  Are sending out signals, and call o'er and o'er,
  Step into the life-boat, be saved evermore,
    O come and trust to Jesus in the life-boat.

7 How grandly the life-boat is riding the waves,
  The shock of the tempest it fearlessly braves,
  Who trust it entirely will find that it saves,
    For Christ is saving sinners in the life-boat.

8 When into the haven we joyously ride,
  The lights of the city will brighten the tide,
  We'll answer the shouts of the saints glorified,
    All glory be to Jesus for his life-boat.

Will the Waters Be Chilly.

I. WATTS.

Arr. by W. J. K.

CHORUS.

1. { Show pit - y, Lord, O Lord, forgive; Prepare me, Lord, to die, }
   { Let a re-pent-ing reb-el live, Prepare me, Lord, to die. } Will the

2. { Are not thy mercies large and free? Prepare me, Lord, to die, }
   { May not a sinner trust in thee? Prepare me, Lord, to die. }

1st.

2d.

waters be chilly? Will the waters be chilly? When I am called to die.

3 My sins are great, but don't surpass,
  Prepare me, Lord, to die;
The power and glory of thy grace;
  Prepare me, Lord, to die.

4 Great God, thy nature hath no bound,
  Prepare me, Lord, to die;
So let thy pard'ning love be found,
  Prepare me, Lord, to die.

5 O wash my soul from every sin,
  Prepare me, Lord, to die;
And make my guilty conscience clean
  Prepare me, Lord, to die.

6 Here on my heart the burden lies,
  Prepare me, Lord, to die;
And past offences pain my eyes,
  Prepare me, Lord, to die.

Blessed Jesus.

Jno. R. Sweney.

Slow, with feeling.

1. Now the solemn shadows darken, And the daylight slowly dies,
2. Some are tried with doubts and dangers, Some have found their hearts grow cold,
3. Some in con - flict sore have striven, With tempta - tion fierce and strong,

Ho - ly Saviour, Thou wilt hearken When thy children's prayers arise.
Some are al - iens now, and strangers To the faith they loved of old.
Lord, to them let strength be giv - en If the bat - tle should be long.

REFRAIN.

Blessed Je - sus, blessed Je - sus, Look on us with loving eyes,
Blessed Je - sus, blessed Je - sus, Bring them back in - to the fold,
Blessed Je - sus, blessed Je - sus, Change their mourning in-to song,

Blessed Je - sus, blessed Je - sus, Look on us with loving eyes
Blessed Je - sus, blessed Je - sus, Bring them back in - to the fold
Blessed Je - sus, blessed Je - sus, Change their mourning in- to song

4 By thy passion in the garden,
   By thine anguish on the tree,
   By that precious gift of pardon
   Won for us alone by thee.

REF.—Blessed Jesus, blessed Jesus,
   Set the sin-bound captives free.

5 When our earthly day is closing,
   And the night grows still and deep,
   Let us, in thine arms reposing,
   Feel thy power to save and keep.

REF.—Blessed Jesus, blessed Jesus,
   Give thine own beloved sleep.

I'm Not Alone.

Mary B. Peck.　　　　　　　　　　　　　　　John E. Kurzenknabe.

1. When darkening shadow 'round me falls, And light and hope seem gone,
2. His eye can pierce the darkest cloud, His arm all danger stay;
3. When sorrows come with crushing blow, O'er my defenceless head;
4. So, cheerfully I'll trav-el on Through life's dark, thorny way;

There is one thought my heart upholds; It is, I'm not a-lone.
He waits for neither look nor word, Our troubles to al-lay.
I tremble not; for well I know Who by my side doth tread.
I'll fear no ill, I'm not a-lone While Je-sus is my stay.

REFRAIN.

No,　　　　nev-er a-lone, Can Je-sus' followers be;
No, not a-lone,

He's ev-er near, why should we fear? Our Guide and Hope is He.

264 Mercy is Boundless and Free.

Henrietta E Blair.   W. J. Kirkpatrick.

1. Thanks be to Jesus, his mercy is free,   Mercy is free,   mercy is free;
2. Why on the mountains of sin wilt thou roam? Mercy is free,   mercy is free;
3. Think of his goodness, his patience, and love, Mercy is free,   mercy is free;
4. Yes, there is pardon for all who believe, Mercy is free,   mercy is free;

REF.—Jesus the Saviour is looking for thee, looking for thee, looking for thee;

Fine.

Sin-ner, that mercy is flowing for thee, Mercy is boundless and free.
Gently the Spirit is calling "Come home," Mercy is boundless and free.
Pleading thy cause with his Father above, Mercy is boundless and free.
Come and this moment a blessing receive, Mercy is boundless and free

Loving- ly, tender - ly calling for thee, Calling and looking for thee.

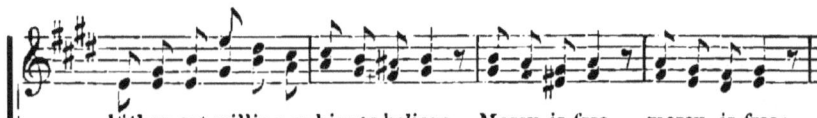

If thou art willing on him to believe, Mercy is free,   mercy is free;
Thou art in darkness, O, come to the light, Mercy is free,   mercy is free;
Come and repenting, O, give him thy heart, Mercy is free,   mercy is free;
Jesus is waiting, O, hear him proclaim, Mercy is free,   mercy is free;

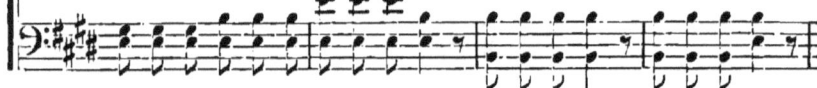

D. C. Refrain.

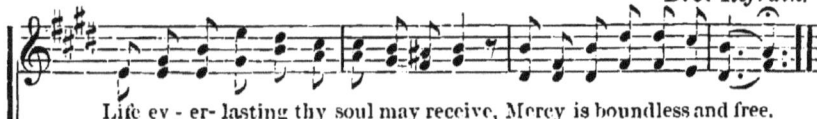

Life ev - er- lasting thy soul may receive, Mercy is boundless and free.
Je-sus is waiting, he'll save you to-night, Mercy is boundless and free.
Grieve him no longer, but come as thou art, Mercy is boundless and free.
Cling to his mercy, believe on his name, Mercy is boundless and free.

Our Cause is Marching On.

Mrs. Fannie H. Carr.

Jno. R. Sweney.

1. We've joined the glorious sisterhood, two hundred thousand strong. With
2. We've heard the cry of childhood, and the prayer of woman too; We've
3. With Jesus for our Captain, no ill can us betide; In the
4. With his light upon our pathway and his grace within our heart Fearing
5. A better day is dawning, the hour is drawing near, King

heart and hand united for the overthow of wrong; With
seen the fall of manhood, and what alcohol will do; We've
secret of his power we assuredly confide; Anchored
naught that man can do to us, nor dreading Satan's dart, Leaning
Alcohol shall be dethroned, with all that he holds dear, And

purpose firm and courage high our phalanx moves along, Our cause is marching on.
consecrated heart and hand to push this campaign through, Our cause is marching on.
to the Rock of Ages securely we abide, Our cause is marching on.
hard on our beloved, from whose strength we ne'er shall part, Our cause is marching on.
peace and plenty crown our land, spreading ev'rywhere, Our cause is marching on.

CHORUS.

Glory, hallelujah! Sing glory, halle-
Glory, glory, hallelujah! Glory, glory, glory, halle-

lujah! Sing glory, hallelujah! Our cause is marching on!
lujah! Glory, glory, hallelujah!

What will the First Greeting be?

P. H. Dingman

Jno. R. Sweney.

1. I have heard of a land, of a beau - ti - ful land, That is
2. Oh, I know that my Sav - iour has gone to pre - pare In his
3. Man - y loved ones have gone to that bright, hap - py land, But their
4. When I pass through the vale of the sha - dow of death To that

o - ver the dark roll-ing sea, And I know there are joys that are
king-dom a man - sion for me, And I know there's a crown and a
fac - es a - gain I shall see, And we'll clasp their glad hands on that
land where the wea - ry are free, I shall join in the song of the

CHORUS.

wait - ing me there,—But what will the first greet-ing be? There'll be
robe and a song,—But what will the first greet-ing be?
beau - ti-ful strand,—But what will the first greet-ing be?
pur - ified throng,—But what will the first greet-ing be?

mu - sic, there'll be singing, And throughout all heaven ringing There'll be

shouts of halle - lujah o'er and o'er; But I know the first to meet me, And with welcome smile to greet me, Will be Jesus when I reach the golden shore.

Hear and Answer Prayer.

FANNY J. CROSBY.   WM. J. KIRKPATRICK.

1. I am pray - ing, bless- ed Sav - iour, To be more and more like thee;
2. I am pray - ing, bless- ed Sav - iour, For a faith so clear and bright
3. I am pray - ing to be hum - bled By the power of grace di - vine,
4. I am pray - ing, bless- ed Sav - iour, And my constant prayer shall be

I am pray - ing that thy Spir - it Like a dove may rest on me.
That its eye will see thy glo - ry Thro' the deep - est, dark - est night.
To be clothed up - on with meekness, And to have no will but thine.
For a per - fect con - se - cra - tion, That shall make me more like thee.

CHORUS.

Thou who know- est all my weak-ness, Thou who knowest all my care,

While I plead each precious promise, Hear, oh, hear and answer prayer.

Just Ahead.

Edgar Page. Cho. by H. L. G.   H. L. Gilmour.

1. 'Mid the toil and the bat - tle I think of my home, Where the
2. By the bank of life's riv - er our loved we shall greet, With
3. There cher - ubs ef - ful - gent and ser - aphs that blaze May
4. As year af - ter year shall fly swift - ly a - way, And
5. Pre - pare, then, ye faith - ful, to en - ter your land, The

sound of life's conflict can nevermore come, Where the angel of peace spreads his
them shall rejoice in a rapture complete, Shall join in the song that the
join in our anthem of rapturous praise; And the Son that was given the
yet but begun is e - ter - nity's day, While springs of new pleasure de-
mansion prepared by the Saviour's own hand, 'Tis read - y, now waiting, so

wings o'er the scene, And e - ter - ni - ty's sea is all calm and se - rene.
glo - ri - fied sing, While the arches of heav - en shall tremble and ring.
world to redeem, Shall be of our joy - ing and praising the theme.
light - eth the soul, While on - ward, yet on - ward, the ag - es shall roll.
beauteous and fair! Then bind on your san - dals, we soon shall be there.

CHORUS.

Just a-head, just a-head a - head, I see the pearl - y

gates unfold. And hear the harps of shining gold, Where blood-bought saints the new song sing To him who redeemed us, our bless - ed King.

On the Way.

Lizzie Edwards.   Jno. R. Sweney.

1. O, bless the Lord, what joy is mine! What perfect peace thro' grace divine!
2. O, bless the Lord, he dwells with me, The voice I hear, the hand I see
3. O, bless the Lord for what I know Of heavenly bliss while here below!
4. O, bless the Lord 'twill not be long Till I shall join the ho- ly throng,

Fine.

And now to realms of end - less day, O, bless the Lord, I'm on the way.
Renew my strength from day to day While home to him I'm on the way.
My trusting heart thro' faith can say, To mansions bright I'm on the way.
And shout and sing thro' endless day, Where every tear is wiped a - way.

D. S.— crown to wear in end - less day, O, bless the Lord, I'm on the way.

CHORUS.   *D S.*

I'm on the way, I'm on the way, In vain the world would bid me stay: A

I Am Safe.

F. A. B.

F. A. BLACKMER.

1. Oft when tossed on ocean's foam, As I voyage to my home,
2. He can cheer the darkest night, He can flood the soul with light,
3. Knowing this I courage take; He will nev - er me forsake,

And no ray of light about I see; With my bark the sport of wave,
He can scatter all our fears a - way; He will hear the honest cry,
But my tri - als help me bear instead; They are on - ly for my good,

When no human arm can save, Un - to Je - sus in my fear I flee.
And all needed grace supply, Sending answers e - ven while we pray.
And when all is understood I shall thank him for the way he led.

CHORUS.

What tho' mountain billows threaten, and the clouds above me roll? I am

safe if Jesus only of my bark shall take control; I can brave the wildest tempest if his glory fills my soul, I can sing amid its raging and rejoice.

A Heart from Sin set Free.

CHAS. WESLEY. L. L. PICKETT.

1. O for a heart to praise my God, A heart from sin set free;
2. A heart resigned, submissive, meek, My great Redeemer's throne;
3. O for a low - ly, contrite heart, Believ - ing, true, and clean,

A heart that al - ways feels thy blood, So free - ly spilt for me.
Where on - ly Christ is heard to speak, Where Je - sus reigns a - lone.
Which neither life nor death can part From him that dwells within!

CHORUS.

A heart from sin set free, 'Tis of thy grace divine; O Lord, I know 'tis

all for me, The glory shall be thine.

4 A heart in every thought renewed,
   And full of love divine:
Perfect, and right, and pure, and good,
   A copy, Lord, of thine.

5 Thy nature, gracious Lord, impart;
   Come quickly from above;
Write thy new name upon my heart,
   Thy new, best name of Love.

Happy Tidings.

Lizzie Edwards.

Jno. R. Sweney.

1. Tidings, happy tidings, Hark! hark! the sound! Hear the joyful e - cho
2. Tidings, happy tidings, Hark! hark! they say, Do not slight the warning,
3. Tidings, happy tidings, Hark! hark! a - gain! Rushing o'er the mountain.

Thro' the world resound; Christ the Lord proclaims them, Hear and heed the call,
Come, oh, come to-day; Christ, our lov - ing Sav - iour, Still repeats the call,
Sweeping o'er the plain; Onward goes the message, 'Tis the Saviour's call,

Come, ye starving ones that perish, Room, room for all. Whoso- ev - er ask - eth,
Come, ye weary, hea- vy- laden, Room, room for all.
Come, for ev'rything is ready, Room, room for all.

REFRAIN.

Jesus will receive; Whosoever thirsteth, Jesus will relieve; See the living

waters, Flowing full and free; Oh, the blessed whosoever! That means me.

DO RE MI FA SO LA TI

Bringing in the Sheaves.

Words from "Songs of Glory."

Geo. A. Minor.

1. Sowing in the morning, sowing seeds of kindness, Sowing in the noon-tide,
2. Sowing in the sunshine, sowing in the shadows, Fearing neither clouds nor
3. Go, then, ev-er weeping, sowing for the Master, Tho' the loss sustained our

and the dew-y eves; Waiting for the har-vest, and the time of reap-ing,
winter's chilling breeze; By and by the har-vest, and the la-bor end-ed,
spir-it oft-en grieves; When our weeping's over, he will bid us welcome,

CHORUS.

We shall come re-joic-ing, bringing in the sheaves. Bringing in the sheaves,

bringing in the sheaves, bringing in the sheaves,
We shall come rejoicing, Bringing in the sheaves,

bringing in the sheaves, We shall come rejoic-ing, bringing in the sheaves,

By permission.

DO RE MI FA SO LA SI

Are You Ready?

MARY D. JAMES.

JNO. R. SWENEY.

1. Should the summons, quickly fly - ing, On the slumb'ring nations fall,—
2. What if now the startling man - date Should the sleeping virgins hear,—
3. Is there oil in all your ves - sels? Are your garments pure and white?
4. Rise! ye vir- gins,—sleep no long - er,—Lest the call your souls surprise!

Lo! the heavenly Bridegroom com- eth, Would the sound your souls appal?
Are your lamps all trimm'd and burning? Should the Bridegroom now appear?
Are they wash'd in-the cleansing fountain, Fit to stand in Je - sus' sight?
Lest ye fail to meet the Bridegroom, When he cometh from the skies.

CHORUS.

Are you read - y? Are you read - y? Should you hear the midnight call?
Are you read - y? Are you read - y? Now to see your Lord ap - pear!
Are you read - y? Are you read - y? Are your lamps all clear and bright?
Oh, be read - y! Oh, be read - y! When he cometh from the skies;

Are you read - y? Are you read - y? Should you hear the midnight call?
Are you ready? Are you ready? Should you hear the midnight call? Should you hear the midnight call?

Are you read - y? Are you read - y? Now to see your Lord appear?
Are you ready? Are you ready? Now to see your Lord appear? Now to see your Lord ap - pear?

Are you read - y? Are you read - y? Are your lamps all clear and bright?
Are you ready? Are you ready? Are your lamps all clear and bright? Are your lamps all clear and bright?

Oh, be read - y! Oh, be read - y! Hasten, from your slumbers rise!
Oh, be ready! Oh, be ready! Hasten, from your slumbers rise! Hasten, from your slumbers rise!

Jesus Saves.

Priscilla J. Owens.   Wm. J. Kirkpatrick.

1. We have heard a joy-ful sound, Je-sus saves, Je-sus saves;
2. Waft it on the roll-ing tide, Je-sus saves, Je-sus saves.
3. Sing a-bove the bat-tle's strife, Je-sus saves, Je-sus saves;
4. Give the winds a might-y voice, Je-sus saves, Je-sus saves,

Spread the glad-ness all a-round, Je-sus saves, Je-sus saves;
Tell to sin-ners, far and wide, Je-sus saves, Je-sus saves;
By his death and end-less life, Je-sus saves, Je-sus saves;
Let the na-tions now re-joice, Je-sus saves, Je-sus saves;

Bear the news to ev-'ry land, Climb the steeps and cross the waves,
Sing, ye is-lands of the sea, E-cho back, ye o-cean caves,
Sing it soft-ly thro' the gloom, When the heart for mer-cy craves,
Shout sal-va-tion full and free, High-est hills and deep-est caves,

Onward, 'tis our Lord's command, Je-sus saves, Je-sus saves.
Earth shall keep her ju-bi-lee, Je-sus saves, Je-sus saves.
Sing in tri-umph o'er the tomb, Je-sus saves, Je-sus saves.
This our song of vic-to-ry, Je-sus saves, Je-sus saves.

DO RE MI FA SO LA SI

Sinner, Turn.

Chas Wesley.

Jno R. Sweney.

1. Sin - ners, turn; why will ye die? God your Mak-er asks you why;
2. Sin - ners, turn; why will ye die? God your Saviour asks you why;
3. Sin - ners, turn; why will ye die? God the Spir - it asks you why;

God, who did your be - ing give, Made you with him - self to live;
He who did your souls retrieve, Died him - self that ye might live.
He who all your lives hath strove, Wooed you to em - brace his love.

He the fa - tal cause demands; Asks the work of his own hands,
Will ye let him die in vain? Cru - ci - fy your Lord a - gain?
Will ye not his grace re - ceive? Will ye still re - fuse to live?

Why, ye thankless creatures, why Will ye cross his love, and die?
Why, ye ransomed sin - ners, why Will ye slight his grace and die?
Why, ye long-sought sin - ners, why Will ye grieve your God and die?

CHORUS.   1st. Rep. pp. 2d.

Sinner, turn; O sinner, turn; Turn, O turn, why will you die? will you die?

Mrs. Phoebe Palmer.　　　　　　　　　　　　Mrs. J. F. Knapp. By per.

1. Oh, when shall I sweep thro' the gates, The scenes of mortal - i - ty o'er,
2. When from Calvary's mount I arise, And pass through the portals above,
3. Yes, loved ones who knew me below, Who learned the new song with me here,
4. The beau - ti - ful gates will unfold, The home of the blood-washed I'll see,
5. A 'sin- ner made whiter than snow, I'll join in the might- y ac- claim,

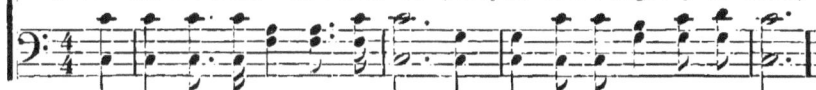

What then for my spir-it awaits? Will they sing on the beauti-ful shore,—
Will shouts, "Welcome home to the skies," Resound through the regions of love?
In cho- rus will hail me, I know, And welcome me home with good cheer.
The cit - y of saints I'll behold, For O, there's a welcome for me!
And shout through the gates as I go, Sal - va- tion to God and the Lamb!

REFRAIN.

Welcome home!　　Welcome home!　　A welcome in glo - ry for
Welcome home,　　　　　Welcome home,

me;　Welcome home! Welcome home!　A welcome for me.
Welcome home,　　Welcome home,　　Welcome home.

Stepping in the Light.

L. H. EDMUNDS.   W. J. KIRKPATRICK.

1. Trying to walk in the steps of the Saviour, Trying to follow our
2. Pressing more closely to him who is leading, When we are tempted to
3. Walking in footsteps of gen-tle forbearance, Footsteps of faithfulness,
4. Trying to walk in the steps of the Saviour, Upward, still upward we'll

Saviour and King; Shaping our lives by his blessed ex-am-ple,
turn from the way; Trusting the arm that is strong to defend us,
mer-cy, and love, Looking to him for the grace free-ly promised,
fol-low our Guide, When we shall see him, "the King in his beauty,"

CHORUS.

Happy, how happy, the songs that we bring. How beautiful to walk in the
Happy, how happy, our praises each day.
Happy, how happy, our journey above.
Happy, how happy, our place at his side.

steps of the Saviour, Stepping in the light, Stepping in the light; How

beautiful to walk in the steps of the Saviour, Led in paths of light.

Tell Me the Story of Jesus.

FANNY J. CROSBY.　　　　　　　　　　　　　　　JNO. R. SWENEY.

1. Tell me the sto - ry of Je - sus, Write on my heart ev -'ry word,
2. Fasting, a - lone in the des - ert, Tell of the days that he passed,
3. Tell of the cross where they nailed him, Writhing in anguish and pain;

CHO.—Tell me the sto - ry of Je - sus, Write on my heart ev'ry word,

Fine.

Tell me the sto - ry most precious, Sweetest that ev - er was heard;
How for our sins he was tempted, Yet was triumphant at last;
Tell of the grave where they laid him, Tell how he liv - eth a - gain;

Tell me the sto - ry most precious, Sweetest that ev - er was heard.

Tell how the angels, in cho - rus, Sang as they welcomed his birth,—
Tell of the years of his la - bor, Tell of the sorrow he bore,
Love in that sto - ry so ten - der, Clear - er than ev - er I see;

D. C.

Glo - ry to God in the high - est! Peace and good tidings to earth.
He was despised and af - flict - ed, Homeless, reject - ed and poor.
Stay, let me weep while you wisper, Love paid the ransom for me.

Draw Me to Thee.

FANNY J. CROSBY.   W. J. KIRKPATRICK.

1. Out on the midnight deep Hear thou my cry, Come to my rescue, Lord,
2. Hope of the des - olate, Light of the soul, Now of my lonely bark
3. Lord, at the open door Let me come in, Heal thou my broken heart,

Save or I die. Let not the stormy waves Break o -ver me,
Take thou control. Yon- der the Ark of Grace Dimly I see,
Wea - ry of sin. Close to thy bleeding side Still would I be,

CHORUS.

Reach out thy loving arm, Draw me to thee. Draw me to thee, Saviour,

Draw me to thee, Reach out thy loving arm, Draw me to thee.

Harvest Time.

W. A. S.

Rev. W. A. Spencer.

1. The seed I have scattered in spring-time with weeping, And watered with
   An-oth-er may shout when the harvesters reaping Shall gath-er my

tears and with dews from on high; ‖ grain in the "sweet by and by."

CHORUS.

O - ver and o - ver, yes, deep - er and deep-er My heart is pierced

D. S.— tears of the sow - er and songs of the reap - er Shall min - gle to-

Fine.

through with life's sorrow-ing cry, But the ‖ gether in joy by and by.

D. S.

By and by, by and by, By and by, by and by, Yes, the

2 Another may reap what in spring-time I've planted,
  Another rejoice in the fruit of my pain,—
  Not knowing my tears when in summer I fainted
  While toiling sad-hearted in sunshine and rain.

3 The thorns will have choked, and the summer sun blasted
  The most of the seed which in spring-time I've sown;
  But the Lord who has watched while my weary toil lasted
  Will give me a harvest for what I have done.

Tell it Out.

Frances R. Havergal.   R. M. McIntosh.   By per.

1. Tell it out among the nations that the Lord is King!
2. Tell it out among the nations that the Saviour reigns!
3. Tell it out among the nations Jesus reigns above!

Tell it out! Tell it out!

Tell it out! Tell it out!

Tell it out among the heathen, bid them
Tell it out among the heathen, bid them
Tell it out among the heathen that his

shout and sing;
break their chains!
reign is love!

Tell it out! Tell it out! Tell it out!

Tell it out with ador-
Tell it out among the
Tell it out among the

a - tion that he shall increase, That the mighty King of glory is the
weeping ones that Je - sus lives! Tell it out among the weary ones what
highways and the lawns at home; Let it ring across the mountains and the

King of peace;
rest he gives;
ocean's foam;

Tell it out! Tell it out! Tell it out! Tell it out!

Tell it
Tell it
Like the

out with jubilation, let the songs ne'er cease;
out among the sinners that he came to save;
voice of many waters let our glad shout be; } Tell it out! Tell it out! Tell it out!

What Must I Do to be Saved?

"Believe on the Lord Jesus Christ, and thou shalt be saved."
Acts xvi. 31.

E. E. HEWITT.   L. L. PICKETT.

1. O, what must I do to be saved From the guilt and dominion of sin? From its
2. O, what must I do to be saved? For the moments are fast gliding by; For e-
3. O, what must I do to be saved? Let me turn unto God's blessed book; For it
4. O, this I must do to be saved! I will come to the Saviour this hour; I will

[within?
fetters and chains, From its manifold stains, Who will free me? Who cleanse me
ternity's near, The great judgement I fear; Soon the summons will come from on high.
bids me "believe," And salvation receive, While on Jesus, Redeemer, I look.
come to his cross, And all else count but dross, I will yield to his life-giving power.

CHORUS.

O, what must I do? what must I do? O, what must I do to be saved?

Jesus, Lover of My Soul.

CHAS. WESLEY.   L. L. PICKETT.

DUET OR QUARTET.

1. Je - sus, Lov - er of my soul, Let me to thy bos - om fly, While the
2. Oth - er ref - uge have I none; Hangs my helpless soul on thee: Leave, O
3. Thou, O Christ, art all I want; More than all in thee I find; Raise the
4. Plenteous grace with thee is found, Grace to cover all my sin: Let the

TUTTI.

near - er wa - ters roll, While the tempest still is high! Hide me,
leave me not a - lone, Still sup - port and comfort me; All my
fall - en, cheer the faint, Heal the sick, and lead the blind. Just and
heal- ing streams abound; Make and keep me pure with- in. Thou of

O my Saviour, hide, Till the storm of life is past; Safe in - to the ha - ven
trust on thee is stayed, All my help from thee I bring; Cover my defenseless
ho - ly is thy name, I am all unrighteousness: False and full of sin I
life the fountain art, Freely let me take of thee; Spring thou up within my

ad lib. . . . .

guide, O receive my soul at last, O receive my soul at last!
head With the shadow of thy wing, With the shadow of thy wing!
am, Thou art full of truth and grace, Thou art full of truth and grace.
heart, Rise to all e - ter - ni - ty, Rise to all e - ter - ni - ty.

Rev. W. Hunter.   T. C. O'Kane.

1. There is a place where the angels dwell, A pure and a peaceful abode;
2. There is a place where they never die, Where beauty and youth never fade;
3. There is a place where my friends have gone Who suffered and worshiped with me,
4. There is a place where I hope to live, When life and its labors are o'er,—

The joys of that place no tongue can tell, But there is the palace of God.
Where never is heard the mournful cry, "My friend, my beloved is dead."
Ex-alted with Christ, high on his throne, The King in his beauty they see.
A place which the Lord to me will give, And then I shall sorrow no more.

CHORUS.

I'm bound for home, for my father-land, The house and the city a-bove; And

rit.

soon shall I join the ransom'd band, And dwell in that city of love.

By permission.

Come, ye Sinners.

JOSEPH HART. JNO. R. SWENEY.

1. Come, ye sin-ners, poor and need-y, Weak and wounded, sick and sore;
2. Now, ye need-y, come and welcome; God's free bounty glo-ri-fy;
3. Come, ye wea-ry, heav-y-la-den, Bruised and mangled by the fall;
4. Lo! th'incarnate God, ascend-ing, Pleads the mer-it of his blood:

Je-sus read-y stands to save you, Full of pi-ty, love, and power;
True be-lief and true repent-ance, Ev-'ry grace that brings you nigh,
If you tar-ry till you're better, You will nev-er come at all;
Ven-ture on him, ven-ture free-ly; Let no oth-er trust in-trude;

He is a - - ble, He is will - - ing, He is a-ble, He is
He is a - ble, He is a - ble, He is willing, He is willing,
Without mon - - ey, Without mon - - ey, Without money, Come to
Not the right - - eous, Not the right - eous, Not the righteous,—Sinners
None but Je - - sus, None but Je - - sus, None but Je-sus Can do

will-ing: doubt no more; . . . He is a - - ble, He is
doubt no more; He is a - ble, He is a - ble, He is
Je-sus Christ and buy; . . . Without mon - - ey, Without
Je-sus came to call; . . . Not the right - - eous, Not the
helpless sin-ners good; . . . None but Je - - sus, None but

will - - ing, He is a - ble, He is willing: doubt no more.
will-ing, He is will-ing, He is will - ing: doubt no more.
mon - - ey, Without money, Come to Jesus Christ and buy.
right - - eous, Not the righteous,—Sinners Jesus came to call.
Je - - sus, None but Je-sus Can do helpless sin-ners good.

Why Don't You Come to Jesus?

For other verses see opposite page. C. R. Dunbar. By per.

1. Come, ye sinners poor and need - y, Weak and wounded, sick and sore;

Je - sus read- y stands to save you, Full of pi - ty, love, and power.

REFRAIN. p   m   f

Why dont you come to Je-sus? He's waiting to receive you, Why

1st. *2d.*

dont you come to Je - sus and be saved? saved?

288 We'll Work till Jesus Comes.

Mrs. Elizabeth Mills.　　Arr. by W. J. K., 1859.　　Dr. Wm. Miller.

CHORUS.

1 O land of rest for thee I sigh,
　When will the moment come,
　When I shall lay my armor by
　And dwell in peace at home?
Cho.—We'll work till Jesus comes,
　We'll work till Jesus comes,
　We'll work till Jesus comes,
　And we'll be gather'd home.

2 No tranquil joys on earth I know,
　No peaceful sheltering dome,

This world's a wilderness of woe,
　This world is not my home.

3 To Jesus Christ I fled for rest;
　He bade me cease to roam,
　And lean for succor on his breast,
　Till he conduct me home.

4 I sought at once my Saviour's side,
　No more my steps shall roam;
　With him I'll brave death's chilling
　And reach my heavenly home. [tide,

289 Happy Land.

Old Melody.

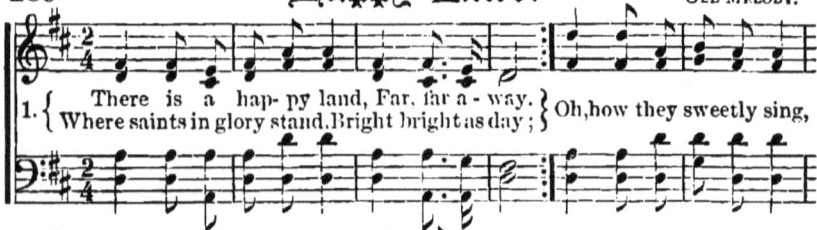

1. { There is a hap-py land, Far, far a-way. }
   { Where saints in glory stand,Bright bright as day; } Oh, how they sweetly sing,

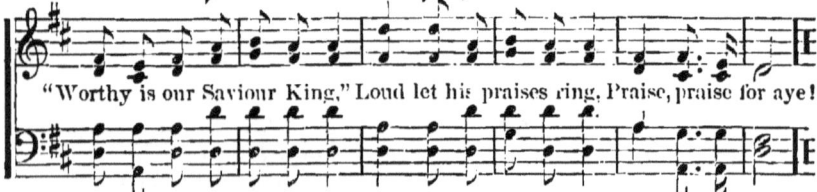

"Worthy is our Saviour King," Loud let his praises ring, Praise, praise for aye!

2 Bright, in that happy land,
　Beams every eye;
　Kept by a Father's hand,
　Love cannot die.
　On, then, to glory run;
　Be a crown and kingdom won;
　And bright, above the sun,
　Reign evermore.

3 Come to that happy land,
　Come, come away;
　Why will you doubting stand?
　Why still delay?
　Oh, we shall happy be.
　When from sin and sorrow free;
　Lord, we shall dwell with thee,
　Blest evermore.

Jesus Saves Me.

Louise M. Rouse.　　　　　　　　　　　　　　　　　Miss Dora Boole.

1. Precious Saviour, thou hast saved me; Thine and only thine I am;
2. Long my yearning heart was trying To en-joy this perfect rest;
3. Trusting, trusting ev'-ry moment; Feeling now the blood applied;
4. Con-se-crat-ed to thy ser-vice, I will live and die to thee:

Oh, the cleansing blood has reached me, Glory, glo-ry to the Lamb!
But I gave all try-ing o-ver: Simply trust-ing. I was blest.
Ly-ing at the cleansing fountain; Dwelling in my Saviour's side.
I will wit-ness to thy glo-ry Of sal-va-tion full and free.

D.S.—Oh, the cleansing blood has reached me, Glory, glo-ry to the Lamb!

REFRAIN.　　　　　　　　　　　　　　　　　　　　　　　　*D.S.*

Glo-ry, glo-ry, Je-sus saves me, Glo-ry, glo-ry to the Lamb!

5 Yes, I will stand up for Jesus;
　　He has sweetly saved my soul,
　Cleansed me from inbred corruption,
　　Sanctified and made me whole.

6 Glory to the blood that bought me,
　　Glory to its cleansing power!
　Glory to the blood that keeps me!
　　Glory, glory, evermore!

291　　　　　　　　I have Sought.　　　　*Tune on opposite page.*

1 I HAVE sought round the verdant earth
　　For unfading joy;
　I have tried every source of mirth,
　　But all, all will cloy;
　Lord, bestow on me
　Grace to set my spirit free;
　Thine the praise shall be,
　　Mine, mine the joy.

2 I have wandered in mazes dark
　　Of doubt and distress;
　I have had not a kindling spark,
　　My spirit to bless;
　Cheerless unbelief
　Filled my lab'ring soul with grief;
　What shall give relief?
　　What shall give peace?

3 Then I turned to thy gospel, Lord,
　　From folly away;
　Then I trusted thy holy word
　　That taught me to pray;
　Here I found release—
　In thy word my soul found peace
　Hope of endless bliss,
　　Eternal day.

4 I will praise now my heavenly King,
　　I'll praise and adore;
　All my heart's richest tribute bring
　　To thee, God of power;
　And in heaven above,
　Saved by thy redeeming love,
　Loud the strains shall move
　　For evermore.

292. I am Coming to the Cross.

Rev. Wm. McDonald.　　　　John vi. 37.　　　　Wm. G. Fischer. By per.

1. I am com - ing to the cross; I am poor, and weak, and blind;
2. Long my heart has sighed for thee, Long has e - vil reigned within;
3. Here I give my all to thee, Friends, and time, and earthly store;

Cho.— I am trust - ing, Lord, in thee, Blest Lamb of Cal - va - ry;

D. C.

I am count - ing all but dross, I shall full sal - va - tion find.
Je - sus sweet - ly speaks to me,— "I will cleanse you from all sin."
Soul and bo - dy thine to be,— Whol - ly thine for ev - er-more.

Humbly at thy cross I bow, Save me, Je - sus, save me now.

4　In thy promises I trust,
　　Now I feel the blood applied:
　I am prostrate in the dust,
　　I with Christ am crucified.

5　Jesus comes! he fills my soul!
　　Perfected in him I am;
　I am every whit made whole:
　　Glory, glory to the Lamb.

293. Rest for the Weary.

Rev. Wm. McDonald.

Rev. S. G. Harmer.

1. In the Christian's home in glo - ry There re - mains a land of rest;
2. Pain or sickness ne'er shall en - ter, Grief nor woe my lot shall share;
3. Death itself shall then be vanquished, And his sting shall be withdrawn:
4. Sing, oh, sing, ye heirs of glo - ry; Shout your triumph as you go;

There my Saviour's gone be - fore me, To ful - fil my soul's request.
But in that ce - les - tial cen - tre, I a crown of life shall wear.
Shout for gladness, O ye ransomed! Hail with joy the ris - ing morn.
Zi - on's gates will o - pen for you, You shall find an entrance through.

CHORUS.

There is rest for the wea - ry, There is rest for the
On the oth - er side of—Jor - dan, In the sweet fields of

wea - ry, There is rest for the wea - ry, There is rest for you—
E - den, Where the tree of life is blooming, There is rest for you.

WM. P. MACKAY.

Revive us again.

J. J. HUSBAND.

1. We praise thee, O God! for the Son of thy love,
For Jesus who died and is now gone above.

REFRAIN.

1st.

2d.

Hal-le-lujah! thine the glory; Halle-lujah! a-men! Revive us a-gain.

2 We praise thee, O God! for thy Spirit of light,
Who has shown us our Saviour and scattered our night.

3 All glory and praise to the Lamb that was slain,
Who has borne all our sins, and has cleansed every stain.

4 All glory and praise to the God of all grace,
Who has bought us, and sought us, and guided our ways.

5 Revive us again; fill each heart with thy love;
May each soul be rekindled with fire from above.

MARY D JAMES.

All for Jesus.

Arranged.

1st.

2d.

1. { All for Jesus! all for Je - sus! All my being's ransomed powers:
{ All my thoughts, and words, and doings, All my days, and all my hours.
2. { Let my hands perform his bidding, Let my feet run in his ways—
{ Let my eyes see Jesus on - ly, Let my lips speak forth his praise,

1st.

2d.

All for Jesus! all for Je - sus! All my days, and all my hours; hours.
All for Jesus! all for Je - sus! Let my lips speak forth his praise; praise.

3 Since my eyes were fixed on Jesus,
I've lost sight of all besides;
So enchained my spirit's vision,
Looking at the Crucified.
‖: All for Jesus! all for Jesus!
Looking at the Crucified. :‖

4 Oh, what wonder! how amazing!
Jesus, glorious King of kings—
Deigns to call me his beloved,
Lets me rest beneath his wings.
‖: All for Jesus! all for Jesus!
Resting now beneath his wings! :‖

296 Come, Ye Disconsolate.

THOMAS MOORE, alt., and THOS. HASTINGS.   SAMUEL WEBBE.

1. Come, ye disconsolate, where'er ye languish; Come to the mercy-seat, fervently kneel;

Here bring your wounded hearts, here tell your anguish;
Earth has no sorrow that heaven cannot heal.

2 Joy of the desolate, light of the straying,
Hope of the penitent, fadeless and pure,
Here speaks the Comforter, tenderly saying,
"Earth has no sorrow that heaven can-
not cure."

3 Here see the bread of life; see waters
flowing
Forth from the throne of God, pure
from above; [knowing
Come to the feast of love; come, ever
Earth has no sorrow but heaven can
[remove.

297 At the Fountain.

OLD MELODY.

CHORUS.

1 Of him who did salvation bring,
I'm at the fountain drinking,
I could forever think and sing,
I'm on my journey home.

CHO —Glory to God,
I'm at the fountain drinking,
Glory to God,
I'm on my journey home.

2 Ask but his grace and lo! 'tis given,
I'm at the fountain drinking,
Ask and he turns your hell to heaven,
I'm on my journey home.

3 Tho' sin and sorrow wound my soul,
I'm at the fountain drinking,

Jesus, thy balm will make me whole,
I'm on my journey home.

4 Where'er I am, where'er I move,
I'm at the fountain drinking,
I meet the object of my love,
I'm on my journey home.

5 Insatiate to this spring I fly,
I'm at the fountain drinking,
I drink and yet am ever dry,
I'm on my journey home.

CHO.—Glory to God,
I'm at the fountain drinking,
Glory to God,
My soul is satisfied.

298 Happy Day.

P. DODDRIDGE. English Melody.

1. O happy day, that fixed my choice On thee, my Saviour and my God!
Well may this glowing heart rejoice, And tell its raptures all abroad. } Happy

Fine. — *D.S.*

day, happy day,
When Jesus washed my sins away! { He taught me how to watch and pray,
And live rejoicing ev'ry day.

2 O happy bond, that seals my vows
To him who merits all my love !
Let cheerful anthems fill his house,
While to that sacred shrine I move.

3 'Tis done! the great transaction's done!
I am my Lord's, and he is mine :
He drew me, and I followed on,
Charmed to confess that voice divine.

4 Now rest, my long-divided heart;
Fixed on this blissful center, rest;
Nor ever from thy Lord depart;
With him of every good possessed.

5 High heav'n that heard the solemn vow,
That vow renewed shall daily hear,
Till in life's latest hour I bow,
And bless in death a bond so dear.

299 He Came to Save Me.

H E. BLAIR. WM. J. KIRKPATRICK.

1st. — 2d.

1. { When Jesus laid his crown aside, He came to save me ;
When on the cross he bled and died, ... He came to save me.

2. { In my poor heart he deigns to dwell, He came to save me ;
Oh, praise his name, I know it well, ... He came to save me.

REFRAIN.

1st. — 2d.

I'm so glad, I'm so glad, I'm so glad that Jesus came, And grace is free,
He . . . came to save me.

3 With gentle hand he leads me still,
He came to save me ;
And trusting him I fear no ill,
He came to save me.

4 To him my faith with rapture clings,
He came to save me ;
To him my heart looks up and sings,
He came to save me.

300. Oh! 'tis Glory in My Soul.

FLORA L. BEST.　　　　　　　　　　　　　　　　　JNO. R. SWENEY.

1. To thy cross, dear Christ I'm clinging, All my re - fuge and my plea;
2. Long my heart hath heard thee calling, But I thrust a - side thy grace;
3. Love e - ter - nal, light e - ter - nal, Close me safe - ly, sweetly in;

Matchless is thy lov - ing kindness, Else it had not stoop'd to me.
Yet, O boundless con - de - scension, Love is shin - ing from thy face.
Sav - iour, let thy balm of healing, Ev - er keep me free from sin.

CHORUS.

Oh, 'tis glo - ry! oh, 'tis glo - ry! Oh, 'tis glo - ry in my soul,

For I've touch'd the hem of his garment, And his pow'r doth make me whole.

301

ROBERT ROBINSON.　　　　　COME, THOU FOUNT.　　　Tune and Chorus above.

1 COME, thou Fount of every blessing,
　Tune my heart to sing thy grace;
Streams of mercy, never ceasing,
　Call for songs of loudest praise.
Teach me some melodious sonnet,
　Sung by flaming tongues above;
Praise the mount—I'm fixed upon it—
　Mount of thy redeeming love!

2 Here I'll raise mine Ebenezer;
　Hither by thy help I'm come;
And I hope, by thy good pleasure,
　Safely to arrive at home.

Jesus sought me when a stranger,
　Wandering from the fold of God;
He, to rescue me from danger,
　Interposed his precious blood.

3 O to grace how great a debtor
　Daily I'm constrained to be!
Let thy goodness, like a fetter,
　Bind my wandering heart to thee:
Prone to wander, Lord, I feel it,
　Prone to leave the God I love;
Here's my heart, O take and seal it;
　Seal it for thy courts above

Come to Jesus.

1. Come to Je - sus, Come to Je - sus, Come to Je - sus just now, Just

now come to   Jesus, Come to Je - sus just now.

2 He will save you, etc.
3 He is able, etc.
4 He is willing, etc.
5 He is waiting, etc.
6 O believe him, etc.
7 He will bless you, etc.

Glory to His Name.

Rev. E. A. HOFFMAN.   *"I will glorify thy name forevermore."*   Rev. J. H. STOCKTON.

1. Down at the cross where my Saviour died, Down where for cleansing from
2. I am so won- drously sav'd from sin, Je - sus so sweetly a-
3. Oh, precious fountain, that saves from sin, I am so glad I have
4. Come to this fountain, so rich and sweet; Cast thy poor soul at the

sin I cried; There to my heart was the blood applied; Glory to his
bides with-in; There at the cross where he took me in; Glo - ry to his
entered in; There Je- sus saves me and keeps me clean, Glory to his
Saviour's feet; Plunge in to-day, and be made complete; Glo - ry to his

D.S.—There to my heart was the blood applied; Glo - ry to his

Fine. CHORUS.   *D.S.*

name.   Glo - ry to his   name,   Glo - ry to his   name;

DO KE MI FA SO LA SI

304 From Greenland's Icy Mountains.

REGINALD HEBER.

L. L. PICKETT.

1. From Greenland's i - cy mountains, From In - dia's cor - al strand;

Where Af - ric's sun - ny fountains Roll down their gold - en sand;

Fine.

D. S.—call us to de - liv - er Their land from er - ror's chain.

D.S.

From many an ancient riv - er, From many a palm - y plain, They

2 What though the spicy breezes
  Blow soft o'er Ceylon's isle;
Though every prospect pleases,
  And only man is vile:
In vain with lavish kindness
  The gifts of God are strewn;
The heathen in his blindness
  Bows down to wood and stone.

3 Shall we, whose souls are lighted
  With wisdom from on high,
Shall we to men benighted
  The lamp of life deny?

Salvation!—O salvation!
  The joyful sound proclaim,
Till earth's remotest nation
  Has learn'd Messiah's name.

4 Waft, waft, ye winds, his story,
  And you, ye waters, roll,
Till like a sea of glory
  It spreads from pole to pole:
Till o'er our ransom'd nature,
  The Lamb for sinners slain,
Redeemer, King, Creator,
  In bliss returns to reign.

305 Nearer, My God, to Thee.

L. L. PICKETT.

1. Near - er, my God, to thee! Near - er to thee, E'en though it
2. Though like the wan - der - er, The sun gone down, Darkness be
3. There let the way ap - pear, Steps un - to heaven; All that thou

Nearer, My God, to Thee.—CONCLUDED.

be a cross That rais-eth me; Still all my song shall be,
o - ver me, My rest a stone, Yet in my dreams I'd be
send-est me, In mer-cy given; Au - gels to beck-on me

Nearer, my God, to thee, Nearer, my God, to thee, Nearer to thee.

4 Then, with my waking thoughts
  Bright with thy praise,
Out of my stony griefs
  Bethel I'll raise;
So by my woes to be
Nearer, my God, to thee,
  Nearer to thee!

5 Or if, on joyful wing
  Cleaving the sky,
Sun, moon, and stars forgot,
  Upward I fly,
Still all my song shall be,
Nearer, my God, to thee,
  Nearer to thee.

306   O Tell Me no More.

CHO.—I'll drink when I'm dry, I'll drink a supply, I'll drink from the fountain That never runs dry.

1 O tell me no more
  Of this world's vain store,
The time for such trifles
  With me now is o'er;
A country I've found
  Where true joys a-
    bound,
To dwell I'm determined
  On that happy ground.

2 The souls that believe
  In paradise live,
And me in that number
  Will Jesus receive;
My soul, don't delay;
  He calls thee away;
Rise, follow thy Saviour,
  And bless the glad day.

3 No mortal doth know
  What he can bestow,—
What light, strength, and
    comfort,—
Go after him, go;
  Lo, onward I move
To a city above, [drous
None guesses how won-
  My journey will prove.

4 Great spoils I shall win
  From death,hell,and sin,
'Midst outward afflictions
  Shall feel Christ within;
And when I'm to die,
  "Receive me," I'll cry,
For Jesus hath loved me,
  I cannot tell why:

5 But this I do find,
  We two are so joined,
He'll not live in glory
  And leave me behind:
So this is the race [grace,
  I'm running through
Henceforth, till admitted
  To see my Lord's face.

6 And now I'm in care
  My neighbors may share
These blessings: to seek
    them
Will none of you dare?
  In bondage, O why,
And death will you lie,
When one here assures you
  Free grace is so nigh?

297

307 Fill Me Now.

Rev. E. H. Stokes, D.D.

Jno. R. Sweney.

1. Hov-er o'er me, Ho - ly Spir - it; Bathe my trembling heart and brow;
2. Thou can'st fill me, gracious Spir - it, Tho' I can - not tell thee how;
3. I am weakness, full of weakness; At thy sa - cred feet I bow;
4. Cleanse and comfort; bless and save me; Bathe, oh, bathe my heart and brow!

S: *Fine.*

Fill me with thy hal - low'd presence, Come, oh, come and fill me now.
But I need thee, great-ly need thee, Come, oh, come and fill me now.
Blest, di-vine, e - ter - nal Spir - it, Fill with power, and fill me now.
Thou art comfort - ing and sav-ing, Thou art sweet - ly fill - ing now.

D.S. Fill me with thy hal-low'd presence,—Come, oh, come and fill me now.

CHORUS.   *D.S.*

Fill me now, fill me now, Je - sus, come, and fill me now;

308 I'm Happy. 11s.

Fine.   *D.C.*

1 I'm happy, I'm happy,
O wondrous account!
My joys are immortal;
I stand on the mount!
I gaze on my treasure,
And long to be there,
With Jesus and angels,
My kindred so dear.

2 O, who is like Jesus!
He's Salem's bright King!
He smiles, and he loves me,
And helps me to sing:
I'll praise him, I'll praise
Whatever his will, [him
While rivers of pleasure
My spirit doth fill.

3 I find him in singing,
I find him in prayer;
In sweet meditation
He always is there.
My constant companion,
O my we ne'er part!
All glory to Jesus,
He dwells in my heart.

298

Laban. S. M.

309 **A charge to keep I have.**

1 A charge to keep I have,
A God to glorify,
A never-dying soul to save,
And fit it for the sky.

2 To serve the present age,
My calling to fulfill,—
Oh, may it all my powers engage,
To do my Master's will.

3 Arm me with jealous care,
As in thy sight to live;
And oh, thy servant, Lord, prepare,
A strict account to give.

4 Help me to watch and pray,
And on thyself rely,
Assured, if I my trust betray
I shall forever die. —C. Wesley.

310 **My soul, be on thy guard.**

1 My soul, be on thy guard;
Ten thousand foes arise;
The hosts of sin are pressing hard
To draw thee from the skies.

2 Oh, watch, and fight, and pray;
The battle ne'er give o'er;
Renew it boldly every day,
And help divine implore.

3 Ne'er think the victory won,
Nor lay thine armor down:
The work of faith will not be done
Till thou obtain the crown.

4 Fight on, my soul, till death
Shall bring thee to thy God;
He'll take thee, at thy parting breath,
To his divine abode. —G. Heath.

311 **Equip me for the war.**

1 Equip me for the war,
And teach my hands to fight;
My simple, upright heart prepare,
And guide my words aright.

2 Control my every thought,
My whole of sin remove;
Let all my works in thee be wrought,
Let all be wrought in love.

3 O arm me with the mind,
Meek Lamb, that was in thee;
And let my knowing zeal be joined
With perfect charity.

4 With calm and tempered zeal
Let me enforce thy call;
And vindicate thy gracious will,
Which offers life to all. —C. Wesley

312 **Lord, in the Strength of Grace.**

1 Lord, in the strength of grace,
With a glad heart and free,
Myself, my residue of days,
I consecrate to thee.

2 Thy ransomed servant, I
Restore to thee thine own;
And from this moment live or die
To serve my God alone.
—C. Wesley.

COWPER.   Arranged by W. J. K.

1. There is a fountain filled with blood, Drawn from Immanuel's veins, And
2. The dy-ing thief re-joiced to see That fountain in his day, And
3. Thou dy-ing Lamb, thy precious blood Shall never lose its power, Till
4. E'er since by faith I saw the stream Thy flowing wounds supply, Re-

sinners, plunged beneath that flood, Lose all their guilty stains. O Lord, have
there may I, though vile as he, Wash all my sins a - way.
all the ransomed Church of God Are saved to sin no more.
deeming love has been my theme, And shall be till I die.

CHORUS.

mer - cy, O Lord, have mercy, O Lord, have mercy, Have mercy on me.

314   Alas! and did.

1 ALAS! and did my Saviour bleed?
    And did my Sovereign die?
Would he devote that sacred head
    For such a worm as I?

2 Was it for crimes that I have done,
    He groaned upon the tree?
Amazing pity! grace unknown!
    And love beyond degree!

3 Well might the sun in darkness hide,
    And shut his glories in,

When Christ, the mighty Maker, died,
    For man, the creature,'s sin.

4 Thus might I hide my blushing face
    While his dear cross appears;
Dissolve my heart in thankfulness,
    And melt mine eyes to tears.

5 But drops of grief can ne'er repay
    The debt of love I owe:
Here, Lord, I give myself away,—
    'Tis all that I can do.   —I. WATTS.

Azmon. C. M.

CARL GOTTHELF GLASER.

315   Lord, I Believe a Rest Remains.

1 LORD, I believe a rest remains
   To all thy people known;
   A rest where pure enjoyment reigns,
   And thou art loved alone:

2 A rest where all our soul's desire
   Is fixed on things above;
   Where fear, and sin, and grief expire,
   Cast out by perfect love.

3 O that I now the rest might know,
   Believe, and enter in!
   Now, Saviour, now the power bestow,
   And let me cease from sin.

4 Remove this hardness from my heart;
   This unbelief remove:
   To me the rest of faith impart,
   The Sabbath of thy love.

CHARLES WESLEY.

316   **I Can, I Will, I Do Believe.**

[To be sung to "There is a Fountain Filled with Blood," or other C. M. words.]

I can, I will, I do believe, I can, I will I do believe; I

can, I will, I do believe that Je - sus saves me now.

317   **How I Love Jesus.**

Alas! and did my Saviour bleed? And did my Sovereign die? Would he devote that

CHORUS.

sa - cred head For such a worm as I? O how I love Je - sus,

O how I love Je- sus; O how I love Jesus, Because he first loved me.

301

Rock of Ages.

TOPLADY.

Tune, TOPLADY. 7s.

Fine.

1. Rock of A - ges, cleft for me, Let me hide my- self in thee;

D.C.—Be of sin the dou - ble cure, Save from wrath and make me pure.

D.C.

Let the wa - ter and the blood, From thy wounded side which flowed,

2 Could my tears forever flow,
Could my zeal no languor know,
These for sin could not atone;
Thou must save, and thou alone:
In my hand no price I bring;
Simply to thy cross I cling.

3 While I draw this fleeting breath,
When my eyes shall close in death,
When I rise to worlds unknown,
And behold thee on thy throne,
Rock of ages cleft for me,
Let me hide myself in thee.

319 **Whiter than Snow.**

1 DEAR Jesus, I long to be perfectly whole;
I want thee forever to live in my soul;
Break down ev'ry idol, cast out ev'ry foe;
Now wash me, and I shall be whiter than snow.

2 Dear Jesus, let nothing unholy remain;
Apply thine own blood, and extract ev'ry stain;
To have this blest washing I all things forego,
Now wash me, and I shall be whiter than snow.

3 Dear Jesus, come down from thy throne in the skies,
And help me to make a complete sacrifice;
I give up myself, and whatever I know,
Now wash me, and I shall be whiter than snow.

4 Dear Jesus, thou seest I patiently wait;
Come now, and within me a new heart create;
To those who have sought thee thou never said'st, no,
Now wash me, and I shall be whiter than snow.

5 Dear Jesus, For this I most humbly entreat;
I wait, blessed Lord, at thy crucified feet;
By faith, for my cleansing, I see thy blood flow,—
Now wash me, and I shall be whiter than snow.

6 The blessing by faith I receive from above;
O glory! my soul is made perfect in love!
My prayer has prevailed, and this moment I know
The blood is applied,—I am whiter than snow.

320 What a Friend.

1 WHAT a friend we have in Jesus,
All our sins and griefs to bear!
What a privilege to carry
Everything to God in prayer!
O, what peace we often forfeit,
O, what needless pain we bear,
All because we do not carry
Everything to God in prayer!

2 Have we trials and temptations?
Is there trouble anywhere?
We should never be discouraged,
Take it to the Lord in prayer.
Can we find a friend so faithful,
Who will all our sorrows share?
Jesus knows our every weakness,
Take it to the Lord in prayer.

3 Are we weak and heavy-laden,
Cumbered with a load of care?—
Precious Saviour, still our refuge,—
Take it to the Lord in prayer.
Do thy friends despise, forsake thee?
Take it to the Lord in prayer;
In his arms he'll take and shield thee,
Thou wilt find a solace there.

321 Lord, I Care Not for Riches.

1 LORD, I care not for riches,
Neither silver nor gold;
I would make sure of heaven,
I would enter the fold:
In the book of thy kingdom,
With its pages so fair,
Tell me, Jesus my Saviour,
Is my name written there?

CHO.—Is my name written there,
On the page white and fair?
In the book of thy kingdom,
Is my name written there?

2 Lord, my sins they are many,
Like the sands of the sea;
But thy blood, O my Saviour,
Is sufficient for me;
For thy promise is written
In bright letters that glow,
"Though your sins be as scarlet,
I will make them like snow."

3 Oh! that beautiful city,
With its mansions of light,
With its glorified beings,
In pure garments of white;
Where no evil thing cometh
To despoil what is fair,
Where the angels are watching,—
Is my name written there?

322 Work! For the Night is Coming.

1 WORK! for the night is coming;
Work through the morning hours;
Work, while the dew is sparkling;
Work, 'mid springing flowers;
Work, when the day grows brighter;
Work, in the glowing sun;
Work, for the night is coming,
When man's work is done.

2 Work, for the night is coming;
Work through the sunny noon;
Fill brightest hours with labor;
Rest comes sure and soon.
Give every flying minute
Something to keep in store;
Work, for the night is coming,
When man works no more.

323 Oh, Think of the Home.

1 OH, think of the home over there,
By the side of the river of life,
Where the saints, all immortal and fair,
Are robed in their garments of white.

CHO.—Over there, over there,
Oh, think of a home over there!

2 Oh, think of the friends over there,
Who before us the journey have trod,
Of the songs that they breathe on the air,
In their home in the palace of God.

3 My Saviour is now over there, [rest;
There my kindred and friends are at
Then, away from my sorrow and care,
Let me fly to the land of the blest.

4 I'll soon be at home over there,
For the end of my journey I see;
Many dear to my heart, over there,
Are watching and waiting for me.

324 More Love to Thee, O Christ.

1 MORE love to thee, O Christ,
More love to thee!
Hear thou the prayer I make,
On bended knee;
This is my earnest plea,
More love, O Christ, to thee,
More love to thee!

2 Once earthly joy I craved
Sought peace and rest;
Now thee alone I seek,
Give what is best:
This all my prayer shall be,
More love, O Christ, to thee,
More love to thee!

3 Then shall my latest breath
Whisper thy praise;
This be the parting cry
My heart shall raise,
This still its prayer shall be,
More Love, O Christ, to thee,
More love to thee!

Balerma. C. M.

325   **O for a Closer Walk.**

1 O FOR a closer walk with God,
  A calm and heavenly frame;
A light to shine upon the road
  That leads me to the Lamb!

2 Where is the blessedness I knew,
  When first I saw the Lord?
Where is the soul-refreshing view
  Of Jesus and his word?

3 What peaceful hours I once enjoyed!
  How sweet their memory still!
But they have left an aching void
  The world can never fill.

4 Return, O holy Dove, return,
  Sweet messenger of rest!
I hate the sins that made thee mourn,
  And drove thee from my breast.

5 The dearest idol I have known,
  Whate'er that idol be,
Help me to tear it from thy throne,
  And worship only thee.

6 So shall my walk be close with God,
  Calm and serene my frame;
So purer light shall mark the road
  That leads me to the Lamb.
                    WILLIAM COWPER.

327   **How Sweet the Name.**

1 How sweet the name of Jesus sounds
  In a believer's ear!
It soothes his sorrows, heals his wounds
  And drives away his fear.

2 It makes the wounded spirit whole,
  And calms the troubled breast;
'Tis manna to the hungry soul,
  And to the weary, rest.

3 Dear name! the rock on which I build,
  My shield and hiding place;
My never-failing treasure, filled
  With boundless stores of grace!

4 Jesus, my Shepherd, Saviour, Friend,
  My Prophet, Priest, and King,
My Lord, my Life, my Way, my End,
  Accept the praise I bring!

5 I would thy boundless love proclaim
  With every fleeting breath;
So shall the music of thy name
  Refresh my soul in death.
                    JOHN NEWT

---

326   **My Father is Rich in Houses and Lands.**

1 My Father is rich in houses and lands,
He holdeth the wealth of the world in
  his hands!   [gold
Of rubies and diamonds, of silver and
His coffers are full,—he has riches untold.

CHO.—I'm the child of a King,
    The child of a King;
      With Jesus my Saviour
    I'm the child of a King.

2 My Father's own Son, the Saviour of
  men: [of them,
Once wandered o'er earth as the poorest

But now he is reigning forever on high, [by.
And will give me a home in heaven by and

3 I once was an outcast stranger on earth,
A sinner by choice, an alien by birth!
But I've been adopted, my name's written
  down,—   [crown.
An heir to a mansion, a robe, and a

4 A tent or a cottage, why should I care?
They're building a palace for me over
  there!   [sing:
Though exiled from home, yet still I may
All glory to God, I'm the child of a King.

304

Arlington. C. M.

328   **Am I a Soldier.**

1 AM I a soldier of the cross,
  A follower of the Lamb,
And shall I fear to own his cause,
  Or blush to speak his name?

2 Must I be carried to the skies
  On flowery beds of ease,
While others fought to win the prize,
  And sailed through bloody seas?

3 Are there no foes for me to face?
  Must I not stem the flood?
Is this vile world a friend to grace,
  To help me on to God?

4 Sure I must fight, if I would reign;
  Increase my courage, Lord;
I'll bear the toil, endure the pain,
  Supported by thy word.

5 Thy saints in all this glorious war
  Shall conquer, though they die:
They see the triumph from afar,
  By faith they bring it nigh.

6 When that illustrious day shall rise,
  And all thy armies shine
In robes of victory through the skies,
  The glory shall be thine.
                ISAAC WATTS.

330   **When I Can Read My Title.**

1 WHEN I can read my title clear
  To mansions in the skies,
I bid farewell to every fear,
  And wipe my weeping eyes.

2 Should earth against my soul engage,
  And fiery darts be hurled,
Then I can smile at Satan's rage,
  And face a frowning world.

3 Let cares like a wild deluge come,
  Let storms of sorrow fall,
So I but safely reach my home,
  My God, my heaven, my all.

4 There I shall bathe my weary soul
  In seas of heavenly rest,
And not a wave of trouble roll
  Across my peaceful breast.
                ISAAC WATTS.

---

329   **Oh, Bliss of the Purified.**

1 OH, bliss of the purified, bliss of the free,
I plunge in the crimson tide opened for
  me;
O'er sin and uncleanness exulting I stand,
And point to the print of the nails in his
  hand.

CHO.—Oh, sing of his mighty love,
  ‖: Sing of his mighty love, :‖
  Mighty to save.

2 Oh, bliss of the purified, Jesus is mine,
No longer in dread condemnation I pine;
In concious salvation I sing of his grace,
Who lifteth upon me the light of his face,

3 Oh, bliss of the purified, bliss of the
  pure,   [cannot cure;
No wound hath the soul that his blood
No sorrow-bowed head but may sweetly
  find rest,   [breast.
No tears but may dry them on Jesus'

4 O Jesus the Crucified, thee will I sing,
My blessed Redeemer, my God and my
  King;
My soul filled with rapture shall shout
  o'er the grave,
And triumph in death in the "Mighty to
  Save."

I'll Live for Him.

C. R. Dunbar.

1. My life, my love I give to thee, Thou Lamb of God, who died for me;
2. I now believe thou dost receive, For thou hast died that I might live;
3. Oh, thou who died on Cal - va - ry, To save my soul and make me free,

Cho.—I'll live for him who died for me, How happy then my life shall be!

D. C.

Oh, may I ev - er faith-ful be, My Sav-iour and my God!
And now henceforth I'll trust in thee, My Sav-iour and my God!
I con - se-crate my life to thee, My Sav-iour and my God!

I'll live for him who died for me, My Sav- iour and my God!

Faber.

He is Calling.

Arr. by S. J. Vail.

1st. *2d.*

1. { There's a wideness in God's mercy, Like the wideness of the sea : } li - berty.
   { There's a kindness in his justice Which is more than }

CHORUS.

He is call-ing, "Come to me!" Lord, I'll glad-ly haste to thee.

2 There is welcome for the sinner,
And more graces for the good ;
There is mercy with the Saviour;
There is healing in his blood.

3 For the love of God is broader
Than the measure of man's mind;

And the heart of the Eternal
Is most wonderful and kind.

4 If our love were but more simple,
We should take him at his word ;
And our lives would be all sunshine
In the sweetness of our Lord.

333. **Forest. L. M.**

55   **O that my load of sin were gone.**   L.M.

1 O that my load of sin were gone!
  O that I could at last submit
At Jesus' feet to lay it down—
  To lay my soul at Jesus' feet!

2 Rest for my soul I long to find:
  Saviour of all, if mine thou art,
Give me thy meek and lowly mind,
  And stamp thine image on my heart.

3 Break off the yoke of inbred sin,
  And fully set my spirit free;

I cannot rest till pure within,
  Till I am wholly lost in thee.

4 Fain would I learn of thee, my God,
  Thy light and easy burden prove,
The cross all stained with hallowed blood,
  The labor of thy dying love.

5 I would, but thou must give the power;
  My heart from every sin release;
Bring near, bring near the joyful hour,
  And fill me with thy perfect peace.
             —CHAS. WESLEY.

334   **I Will Sprinkle.**   *Fine.*

1. Ye who know your sins forgiv - en, And are hap - py in the Lord,
Have you read that gracious promise, Which is left up - on record?
D. C.—Sanc - ti - fy and make you holy, I will come and dwell within.

REFRAIN.   *D. C.*

I will sprinkle you with wa - ter, I will cleanse you from all sin,

2 Tho' you have much peace and comfort,
  Greater things you yet may find,—
Freedom from unholy tempers,
  Freedom from the carnal mind.

3 Be as holy, and as happy,
  And as useful here below,
As it is your Father's pleasure;
  Jesus, only Jesus know.

4 Spread, O spread the joyful tidings,
  Tell, O tell what God has done,
Till the nations are conformed
  To the image of his Son.

5 O may every soul be filled
  With the Holy Ghost to-day;
He is coming, he is coming;
  O prepare, prepare the way.

Sweet Land of Rest.

1. Sweet land of rest, for thee   I sigh! When will the moment come,
D. C.—And dwell with Christ at home, . . . And dwell with Christ at home;
2. No tran-quil joys on earth I know, No peaceful, sheltering dome;
D. C.—This world is not my home, . . . This world is not my home;

D. C.

When I shall lay my ar - mor by, And dwell with Christ at home.
This world's a wil - der-ness of woe, This world is not my home.

3 To Jesus Christ I sought for rest,
　He bade me cease to roam ;
But fly for succor to his breast,
　And he'd conduct me home.

4 Weary of wand'ring round and round
　This vale of sin and gloom,
I long to leave th'unhallowed ground,
　And dwell with Christ at home.

Only Trust Him.

"Take my yoke upon you, and learn of me; and ye shall find rest unto your souls."—Matt. xi. 29.

J. H. S.　　　Rev. J. H. Stockton. By per.

1. Come, ev'ry soul by sin oppressed, There's mercy with the Lord, And he will surely
2. For Jesus shed his precious blood Rich blessings to bestow; Plunge now into the
3. Yes, Jesus is the Truth, the Way, That leads you into rest; Believe in him with-
4. Come then, and join this holy band, And on to glory go, To dwell in that ce-

CHORUS.

give you rest, By trusting in his word.   On - ly trust him, only trust him,
crimson flood That washes white as snow. *Second Chorus*—
out de-lay, And you are ful-ly blest.   Come to Je-sus, come to Je-sus,
lestial land, Where joys immortal flow.

Only trust him now; He will save you, he will save you, He will save you now.
Come to Jesus now;

337   ## The Great Physician.

REV WM. H. HUNTER. D. D.   Arranged by J H STOCKTON.

1. The Great Phy- si- cian now is here, The sym- pa- thiz ing Je - sus;
He speaks the drooping heart to cheer, Oh, hear the voice of Je - sus.

CHORUS.

Sweet-est note in ser- aph song, Sweetest name on mor- tal tongue,

Sweet-est car - ol ev - er sung, Je - sus, bles- sed Je - sus.

pp

2 Your many sins are all forgiven,
  Oh, hear the voice of Jesus;
Go on your way in peace to heaven,
  And wear a crown with Jesus.

3 All glory to the dying Lamb!
  I now believe in Jesus;
I love the blessed Saviour's name,
  I love the name of Jesus.

4 The children too, both great and small,
  Who love the name of Jesus,
May now accept his gracious call
  To work and live for Jesus.

5 Come, brethren, help me sing his praise,
  Oh, praise the name of Jesus;
Come, sisters. all your voices raise,
  Oh, bless the name of Jesus.

6 His name dispels my guilt and fear,
  No other name but Jesus;
Oh, how my soul delights to hear
  The precious name of Jesus.

7 And when to that bright world above,
  We rise to see our Jesus,
We'll sing around the throne of love
  His name, the name of Jesus.

338 **It is Good to be Here.**

Rev. I. N. Wilson   Jno. R. Sweney, by per.

While we bow in thy name, Oh, meet us a-gain, Fill our
May the Spir-it of grace, And the smiles of thy face, Gent-ly

D. S.—light streaming down makes the pathway all clear, It is

Fine. REFRAIN.

hearts with the light of thy love; } It is good to be here, it is
fall on us now from a-bove. }

good for us, Lord, to be here.

D. S.

good to be here, Thy perfect love now drives a-way all our fear, And

2 Our souls long for thee;
  Oh, may we now see
A sin-cleansing blood-wave appear;
  And feel, as it rolls
  In power o'er our souls,
It is good for us, Lord, to be here.

3 Thou art with us, we know;
  We feel the sweet flow   [tide;
Of the sin-cleansing wave's gladd'ning
  We are washed from our sin,
  Made all holy within,
And in Jesus we sweetly abide.

339   **O how Happy are They.**   *Tune and Chorus above.*

1 O how happy are they
  Who the Saviour obey,
And have laid up their treasures above;
  Tongue can never express
  The sweet comfort and peace
Of a soul in its earliest love.

2 That sweet comfort was mine,
  When the favor divine
I received through the blood of the Lamb;
  When my heart first believed,
  What a joy I received—
What a heaven in Jesus' name!

3 'Twas a heaven below
  My Redeemer to know,
And the angels could do nothing more
  Than to fall at his feet,
  And the story repeat,
And the Lover of sinners adore.

4 Jesus, all the day long,
  Was my joy and my song;
O, that all his salvation might see:
  He hath loved me, I cried,
  He hath suffered and died,
To redeem even rebels like me.

Take me as I am.

ANON.   Rev. J. H. STOCKTON.

1. Je-sus, my Lord, to thee I cry, Unless thou help me I must die;
2. Helpless I am, and full of guilt, But yet for me thy blood was spilt,
3. I thirst, I long to know thy love, Thy full sal-vation I would prove;
4. If thou hast work for me to do, Inspire my will, my heart renew,
5. And when at last the work is done, The bat-tle o'er, the vic-t'ry won,

Fine.

Oh, bring thy free sal - va-tion nigh, And take me as I am!
And thou can'st make me what thou wilt, But take me as I am!
But since to thee I can-not move, Oh, take me as I am!
And work both in and by me, too, But take me as I am!
Still, still my cry shall be a-lone, Oh, take me as I am!

D. S.— bring thy free sal - va-tion nigh, And take me as I am!

REFRAIN.   **D. S.**

Take me as I am,   Take me as I am;   Oh,
Take me, take me as I am, Take me, take me as I am;

DO RE MI FA SO LA SI

JUST AS I AM.   Tune and Chorus above.

1 JUST as I am, without one plea,
  But that thy blood was shed for me,
  And that thou bid'st me come to thee,
    O Lamb of God, I come!

2 Just as I am, and waiting not
  To rid my soul of one dark blot,
  To thee whose blood can cleanse each
    O Lamb of God, I come! [spot,

3 Just as I am, though tossed about
  With many a conflict, many a doubt,
  Fightings within, and fears without,
    O Lamb of God, I come!

4 Just as I am—poor, wretched, blind;
  Sight, riches, healing of the mind,
  Yea, all I need, in thee to find,
    O Lamb of God, I come!

5 Just as I am—thou wilt receive,
  Wilt welcome, pardon, cleanse, relieve;
  Because thy promise I believe,
    O Lamb of God, I come!

6 Just as I am—thy love unknown
  Hath broken every barrier down,
  Now, to be thine, yea, thine alone,
    O Lamb of God, I come!

More Faith in Jesus.

Henrietta E. Blair.   Wm. J. Kirkpatrick.

1. While struggling thro' this vale of tears I want more faith in Je-sus; A-
2. To war against the foes with-in I want more faith in Je-sus; To
3. To brave the storms that here I meet I want more faith in Je-sus; To
4. I want a faith that works by love, A constant faith in Je-sus; A

D. S.—And

Fine. CHORUS.

mid tempta-tions, cares, and fears, I want more faith in Je - sus. I
rise a-bove the powers of sin I want more faith in Je - sus.
rest con-fid-ing at his feet I want more faith in Je - sus.
faith that mountains can remove, A liv-ing faith in Je - sus.

this my cry, as time rolls by, I want more faith in Je - sus.

D. S.

want more faith, I want more faith, A clearer, brighter, stronger faith in Jesus;

Copyright, 1885, by John J. Hood.

Hallelujah! Amen.

Henrietta E. Blair.   Adapted and arr. by Wm. J. Kirkpatrick.

1. How oft in holy converse With Christ, my Lord, alone, I seem to hear the
2. They pass'd thro' toils and trials And tho' the strife was long, They share the victor's
3. My soul takes up the chorus, And pressing on my way, Communing still with
4. Thro' grace I soon shall conquer, And reach my home on high; And thro' e-ternal

CHORUS.

millions That sing around his throne:— Hal-le-lu-jah, a-men. Halle-
conquest, And sing the victor's song.
Je-sus. I sing from day to day:
a-ges I'll shout beyond the sky:

poco rit.

lu-jah, A-men. Hal-le-lu-jah, A-men.   A-men,   A-men.

344   **O Thou in whose.**   Tune.
MEDITATION. 11,8.

JOSEPH SWAIN.   FREEMAN LEWIS, arr. by HUBERT P. MAIN.

1 O thou in whose presence my soul takes
      On whom in affliction I call, [delight.
  My comfort by day and my song in the
      My hope, my salvation, my all! [night,

2 Where dost thou, dear Shepherd, resort
      with thy sheep,
  To feed them in pastures of love?
  Say, why in the valley of death should I
      Or alone in this wilderness rove? [weep,

3 Or why should I wander an alien from
      Or cry in the desert for bread? [thee,
  Thy foes will rejoice when my sorrows they
      And smile at the tears I have shed. [see,

4 Ye daughters of Zion, declare, have you
      The star that on Israel shone? [seen
  Say if in your tents my Beloved has been,
      And where with his flocks he has gone.

5 He looks! and ten thousands of angels
      And myriads wait for his word; [rejoice,
  He speaks! and eternity, filled with his
      Re-echoes the praise of the Lord [voice,

6 Dear Shepherd, I hear, and will follow
      thy call;
  I know the sweet sound of thy voice;
  Restore and defend me, for thou art my all,
      And in thee I will ever rejoice.

Sessions. L. M.

DOXOLOGY.

L. O. EMERSON.

Praise God from whom all blessings flow ; Praise him, all creatures here below,

Praise him above, ye heavenly host, Praise Father, Son   and Ho- ly Ghost.

346

Old Hundred. L. M.

DOXOLOGY.

G. FRANC.

Praise God from whom all blessings flow ; Praise him, all creatures here below ;

Praise him a- bove, ye   heav'nly host, Praise Father, Son and Ho- ly Ghost.

347

Gloria Patri.

1. Glory be to the Father, and to   the   Son,   and   to   the   Ho - ly Ghost;
2. As it was in the begining,
    is now, and   ev - er shall be, world without end. A - men.

INDEX.

Titles in CAPITALS; Metrical Tunes in *Italic*; First lines in Roman.